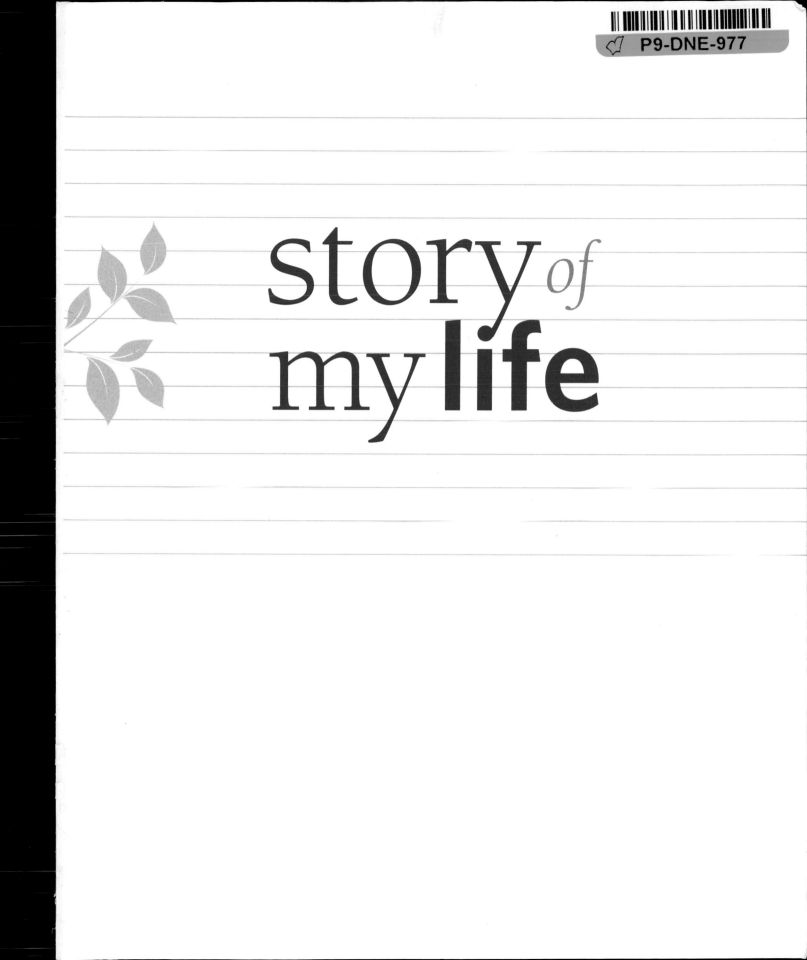

story *of*
my **life**

story *of* my **life**

a workbook for preserving your legacy

SUNNY JANE MORTON

FAMILY TREE BOOKS

CINCINNATI, OHIO
shopfamilytree.com

contents

1

gathering your family stories

We share our life stories for many reasons. We want to make sense of the past or relive cherished memories. We want to set the record straight. We want future generations to know us as we really are and benefit from lessons we've learned. However, writing an entire life story can be intimidating. There is so much to tell—so many details. The project can quickly become overwhelming.

The *Story of My Life* workbook helps you and your loved ones recall and write your life histories in an orderly, step-by-step manner. No need to worry that you won't be able to recall or tell things clearly—you'll get plenty of instruction on reviving your memories and writing them well. Then you'll start filling in genealogical facts, milestone events, and everyday details.

This book also helps you document relationships and values that have shaped your life. Scan and print any section, then send it to someone else—parents, siblings, children, grandchildren, school friends, or neighbors—and ask for their side of the story. The short fill-in format is easy for anyone to complete.

In the end, you'll have a meaningful summary of your life, its lessons, and those who have helped make it special. You'll gain new perspective on past events and relationships. And you will create a priceless keepsake that preserves your personal and family legacy for generations to come.

Answer the questions in each section as best you can. If information is requested that doesn't apply to your situation (such as a marriage date for an unmarried romantic partnership), try to provide an answer of some kind rather than leave the section blank (e.g., *not married* or *moved in together spring 1983*). Where information is unknown, indicate that in pencil. You can erase and replace it with better data if and when you find it. At the top of most pages, you'll find a place to enter the date and the name of the person who filled out the form, if it wasn't you.

Of course, you may not find all sections of this workbook relevant to you. If you didn't go to college, skip over those pages. If you married and had children before entering the workforce as an older adult, you might complete Stories About a Family of Your Own before Stories From Your Professional Life. For events yet to happen in your life, leave the corresponding pages blank, ready for your thoughts when the time comes. Use the flexible Special Forms section to customize your life story, and pay tribute to those who have influenced your life at critical times but aren't related to you: neighbors, coaches, teachers, roommates, and friends. In each section, make liberal use of Special Forms to capture unique and significant aspects of your life.

The introduction to each chapter provides suggestions on how you might use the pages in that section. Find out more about these pages below.

Finally, send lots of forms to others to fill out, but continue working on this book on your own. Your successful completion of this project does not depend on anyone else. Simply record others' memories if and when they return their forms. In the end, you'll have a meaningful summary of your life, its lessons, and those who have helped make it special. You'll gain new perspective on past events and relationships. And you will create a priceless keepsake that preserves your personal and family legacy for generations to come.

Special Forms for Your Special Life

No two families are alike! The Special Forms chapter helps you document unique experiences and relationships. Fill out copies of Special Forms and insert them in the chronological or family section that's most appropriate. Special Forms include:

» **Special People.** Document anyone who made your life more meaningful: a favorite extended family member, godparent, teacher, coach, friend, or neighbor. Send these pages to others and ask them to fill them out for you.

» **Special Places.** Describe the campground your family returned to each summer or the café table that became "yours" during that spring in Paris. Special Places don't have to be exotic: They might be a tree house, back porch, or window seat that was your own little hideaway. Special Places might also be used to describe a favorite uncle's house on the coast of Maine or your great-grandfather's farm in West Virginia where the annual family reunion is held.

» **Special Memories.** Commemorate a religious or cultural rite of passage: a First Communion, baptism, bar mitzvah, sweet-sixteen party, quinceañera, or missionary or Peace Corps service. Document a graduation party, bridal or baby shower, the year your team won the big game, your election to student (or city) council, a promotion, or a loved one's wedding. Or write about those everyday moments that became eternal in your memory: baking with your grandmother, late-night chats with dorm buddies, or the morning coffee ritual with your spouse. Send copies of these pages to loved ones with requests that they share a special memory with you.

» **Life-Changing Experiences.** Honor events that profoundly changed the way you look at the world or yourself. You might use this page to document international travel, volunteer work, missionary service, a brush with serious illness or death, or any other type of momentous experience.

» **Flashbulb Memories.** A "flashbulb memory" is your vivid recollection of a highly public event: the first manned moon landing, the assassination of President Kennedy, the *Challenger* explosion, or the events of September 11, 2001. Where you were, what you were doing, and how you felt tells something about your life and your relationship to the world around you.

» **Memorabilia.** On these pages, adhere copies of documents, photos, postcards, or other images related to that section. Make reduced-sized copies as needed. Caption memorabilia with a description of what it shows and a note stating where the original is. (Valuable original memorabilia should be preserved elsewhere, in an archival environment.)

» **In Memoriam.** Use this page to document and honor the passing of a loved one, whether a stillborn child, dear friend, aged relative, or beloved pet.

How to Remember Your Life

You may wonder how you will possibly remember all the answers to the questions in this book. You won't—at least, not right away. You'll recall some things in vivid detail, like your first car or the last holiday you spent with your father before he died. But memories of equally meaningful experiences may be embarrassingly fuzzy, like the birth of your first child (especially if you were the one giving birth).

The good news is that the simple process of remembering one thing causes more memories to surface. As you work through this book, you will be prompted to recall important events and everyday details. As you start recalling them, you'll remember other things as well. For example, while thinking about your wedding day, you might recall that your best man was your college roommate. Thinking of your roommate may bring to mind a long-forgotten road trip to Las Vegas. Then you may mentally segue to the aunt you once visited in Las Vegas—another story altogether that is connected by the slender mental thread of Las Vegas.

What do you do with the avalanche of disordered memories that begin to pile up? Organize them in the book. Simply skip around to different chronological sections and record thoughts as they occur. If your memories don't coincide with the memory prompts, use Special Forms like Special Memories and Life-Changing Experiences.

Of course, there will still be things you don't remember, but want to. When that happens, try some of these tried-and-true tricks to fill in your memory gaps:

1. Look through old photos, yearbooks, date books, letters or papers, clothing, jewelry, collections, and other memorabilia.

2. Listen to songs that were popular or that you loved during that time period. This is especially effective for re-creating emotional memories.

3. Travel back to the setting of an event or time period. Walk through your old neighborhood, visit your alma mater, or stop at the courthouse where you were married. If you can't go to the actual place, try re-creating the ambiance: Visit any lake beach or urban street with sights, sounds, and smells that may trigger your memory. You might even use the Street View function on Google maps **<maps.google.com>** to take a virtual stroll along your old street.

4. Contact someone who was part of your life and reminisce together. Be considerate about whom you contact; don't call those whose memories of the time in question may be unpleasant or unresolved.

5. Read more about that time period or place in a local history or in books, such as the *Our American Century* series by Time-Life Books.

In the end, you still won't remember every detail—who does? Every additional memory you bring to the surface is well worth the effort.

Optional Exercises

This section is not meant to distract you from documenting your life stories. Rather, it offers optional exercises to improve your recall and the effectiveness of your writing. Turn to these suggestions when you run out of memories or story-telling energy. Write them in a private notebook or computer file so you feel free to make mistakes, explore the truth of memories or feelings, or go on that angry rant (which probably shouldn't end up in the final version of your book).

1. When you run out of memories about a particular time period or person: Across the top of the page, write the subject you're trying to recall (for example, "Grandma"), and then begin the page with "I remember..." Start writing everything you can remember and keep writing for a solid five or ten minutes. Write everything that comes to mind, even if it's not a complete thought or it doesn't make much sense. Record images, names, feelings, addresses, descriptions, etc. When you run out of memories, write "I remember" until you actually have a memory to write.

2. When you are overcome with emotion about a subject: Write an imaginary letter. If your emotion is directed at someone (such as God, fate, or even the post office), write it to them. If your emotion doesn't have a personal target, consider writing an imaginary letter to a good friend. "I am so mad when I think of..." *Do not send this letter.* Just write it and walk away. You may want to destroy it immediately. After you've had time to cool off, return to your writing in the book and see what happens.

3. Write about yourself as if you were an outside observer. Choose the perspective of your roommate, boss, younger sister, or anyone who might have known you well during a particular time. Think through the patterns of your daily life, what you did on the weekends, how you dressed, where you hung out and with whom. Describe yourself as others probably saw you: a grassroots activist, a busy mom, an invalid, a churchgoer, a baseball fan. Then write about how you were or weren't what you appeared to be.

Composite Memories

If you're like most people, you don't recall every birthday or Thanksgiving dinner separately. Rather, you have a "composite memory" of many such occasions during your childhood, with a few stories or details that stand out. Your composite memories give a broad sense of what your life was like, but they can seem too vague without a specific memory attached. Look at the following example (the composite memory comes first, followed by a specific stand-out memory in italics):

> My birthday parties were always noisy with relatives. My cousins sang as I blew out candles, laughed while I opened presents, and screamed around the piñata. *One year, we couldn't get the piñata to break. My father took a baseball bat to it. He spun around so hard he fell on the ground as the piñata finally burst open, and candy showered his head.*

The first two sentences, the composite memory of childhood birthdays, are like an outline drawing. The specific anecdote about the piñata colors in the outline. Use both composite memories and stand-out details to form a more complete and vivid picture of your past.

Filled-In Memories

Sometimes you recall one event that meant a lot to you, but can't recall important details. How can you evoke that special weekend trip with your dad without fudging or guessing at the particulars?

Modern memoirists—the really good ones whose personal stories read like the best novels—aren't bothered by having to reinvent details. They care more about communicating the essence of their experience. But you don't have to take any literary license to combine what you do recall with plausible additions. In the following example, the "plausible additions" are italicized:

> We drove through the Missouri countryside, playing hooky from a history conference. Empty straight highways backdropped our easy conversation. Dad drove. I sat with my feet propped on the dashboard. We traded turns with the cassette deck and preached the merits of music that moved us. *His was probably Eric Clapton and lots of jazz. Mine was likely ninety-minute mixes of contemporary folk music bummed from college roommates' CDs. We likely stopped for convenience-store snacks all afternoon and licked our fingers over homemade barbecue at a small-town diner.* We returned to the conference well after the evening banquet. I remember the deep joy of feeling that my dad wanted only to be with me.

Note that real memories and guesses—which are acknowledged as such—fuse to create a complete memory that others can appreciate. We understand exactly the meaning of this memory.

Joyful Memories

Everyone has moments (often much longer periods) of joy, quiet contentment, personal triumph, or deep satisfaction: times when faith or hard work was rewarded, family or friends came through, or a season of life went smoothly. Make sure this "good news" of life is recorded in each season of your life, either in the regular pages or Special Forms. Your admission of happiness—however brief it may be—allows you to relive it and brings hope and happiness to readers who can share it with you.

Privacy and Painful Memories

You may choose not to include certain events or time periods in your life. You have a right to privacy; recording your life story is not a tell-all confessional! Share only what you want, and omit certain pages or sections. Of course, you may decide at a later date that you want to share those things after all. You may discover, in the process of writing, that your losses or pain taught you lessons or built your character in such a way that you want to share those experiences.

When all is said and done, the most important quality of your memories is not their thoroughness, but their honesty and integrity. Your emotional honesty about complicated feelings and hard-learned lessons—along with all the fun stuff—will make readers love you even more and trust what you have to say.

Stories About Others

Many who write their stories wonder how they will approach negative or unhappy truths that involve their loved ones. Write about your mother's alcoholism? Your father's temper? Will you hurt them? Will you anger your siblings? What if you tell about your own youthful transgressions—will you embarrass your parents or friends?

Everyone will solve this dilemma differently. Some prioritize the tender feelings of loved ones; others feel a moral obligation to truth-telling. (Telling a negative story out of jealousy, spite, vengeful feelings, or even righteous indignation isn't the same as a moral obligation to honesty. Readers can sense intent. If yours is not good, the end result will likely reflect more negatively on you than anyone else.)

You probably don't want your life story to read as either an angry rant or a sappy tale in which no character ever steps out of line. Neither attitude does justice to life's complicated events and relationships. Where you cannot be fair or balanced (and nobody is fair and balanced about everything), just say so: "Even years later, I cannot think of that betrayal without venom in my heart." Your honesty alerts your readers (and yourself) that your feelings are sore and your judgment may not be objective or charitable, keeping the readers' trust in you and allowing them to judge for themselves if they must.

In the end, this is your version of your life—not your mother's version, not your sister's version. Don't feel you speak for your entire family. Whatever stories you choose to tell, tell them how you experienced them, what you thought or felt. This is your turn to talk, so make the most of it.

Enlisting Help

Others who have contributed to your life story can help you write it! There are forms for your parents, siblings, spouse/partner, and children to fill out about themselves and their relationships with you at different times of your life. When they add their unique voices and perspectives, your life's record becomes more dimensional.

You can also request any kind of memories from anyone with the versatile Special Forms. So think of your favorite stories from the past and who would tell them well. Maybe your aunt would retell the tale of your teenage mom driving the car into the river. Ask your brother to write about the time you wrestled each other down the stairs and accidentally punched a hole in the stairwell wall. Send these pages to your loved one with a specific request and a copy of the Special Memories form, then insert his or her completed pages into the appropriate section of this book.

You can also ask people to help fill the gaps in your own knowledge. Perhaps you don't remember your father or the house you lived in when you were five. Ask an older relative to write about your father, or your older sister to recall details about the house.

You might even request the same memories from multiple people. Everyone will remember things differently, and each perspective has value. You and your siblings will recall your childhoods in unique ways. Each high-school roommate or college buddy will have a different take on the times you shared. (Resist the need to try to set the record straight if stories conflict; sometimes the discrepancies are the most interesting and enlightening parts to read!)

To whom might you send pages to fill out? If they are still living, consider your:

1. grandparents and godparents

2. aunts, uncles, and cousins

3. in-laws

4. friends from childhood, school, and adulthood

5. neighbors (past or present)

6. teachers, coaches, counselors, and other mentors

7. coworkers (past or present)

8. members of an organization you belonged to

Some people will respond easily when you ask for help. Others will send something very special only after patient persuasion. Still others may prefer you to interview them, then fill out the form on their behalf. Some of your potential contributors may need to have their memories jogged. Try sending a copy of your own memories of the event in question along with a request for

theirs. Or try the tricks listed earlier in this chapter: Look at old photo albums together or visit your old hangout.

Not sure how to ask someone to participate? Send her an e-mail or message her via a social networking site. State briefly what you're working on, and acknowledge her contribution to your life. Ask her to write her memories from a particular event or time period and send it to you by a specific date to encourage her prompt response.

Here's a sample letter of invitation:

Dear Miriam,

I've been writing some of my life stories lately. I'm working on my college years. I know I've thanked you many times for your friendship, but I'm not sure I ever told you how much I loved and admired you.

I hope to include your voice and memories in my life history. Will you please write down a few memories of our time together on the enclosed form? There's an extra page in case you need more room for your thoughts. I've enclosed an envelope you can return them in.

Thank you for sending this back within the next two weeks or so. If you have any questions, just give me a call or e-mail me at …

When she sends you her responses, you can copy them onto a Special Form and note who the information is from. If she doesn't communicate via computer, you can send a letter with the Special Pages form enclosed. Be sure to include a self-addressed stamped envelope so she can easily mail back the response. Or you could arrange a phone interview or meet in person.

Use the Request for Memories chart on the next page to track your requests to others for their help with this project.

Request for Memories

Use this page to keep track of those you've invited to contribute to your *Story of My Life* workbook project. Noting in which section or chapter you plan to place their comments will help you stay organized and ensure that each section has sufficient contributions.

Name	Page/Topic	Date Sent	Date Received

2

statistics about me

The purpose of this section is to create a record of your major life events, including birth and adoption, family structure, religious rites, residences, education, employment (including military service), memberships, marriages, and children. More details about these events will be requested in future chapters; this section just collects basic life statistics in one place.

Don't let unknown answers halt your progress. As you move forward through each section of the book, you may recall or discover more information that you can add to this chapter.

Find information requested in this section in a variety of sources, such as:

» Birth certificates
» Adoption papers
» Baby books
» Birth announcements
» Family bibles
» Baptismal records
» Church or synagogue records
» Medical records
» Medical bills
» School records and correspondence
» School grade reports and diplomas
» Letters, including envelopes
» Bank statements
» Loan applications
» Mortgage documents
» Lease papers
» Court files
» Job applications
» Pay stubs
» Employment performance reviews
» Résumés
» Government or employment benefits paperwork
» Copies of tax returns and tax documents
» Investment applications and statements
» Military enlistment and discharge papers
» Military benefits statements
» Marriage license applications and certificates
» Divorce papers
» Social security or pension statements
» Family trees and family group sheets

tips

If you need help finding the documents listed on these pages, look carefully through old paperwork. Try looking in these places:

» Check your own files. Don't forget to check the safe!

» Ask others who might have them, especially your parents or siblings. If your parents have passed away, ask whomever handled the estate or emptied their home.

» Request duplicate copies from the originating institution, if possible and practical. Learn more about locating and requesting these records in resources like:

» *The Public Record Research Tips Book: Insider Information for Effective Public Record Research* by Michael Sankey (Facts on Demand Press)

» FamilySearch Research Wiki <familysearch.org/wiki/en/Main_Page>

» *The Family Tree Sourcebook eBook* by the editors of Family Tree Magazine <www.shopfamilytree.com/family-tree-sourcebook-ebook-y3259>

Birth

Natural or birth parents should be listed on this page, if known.

Name

_____

First   Middle   Last   Suffix(es)

Date of Birth

_____

Day   Month   Year

Place of Birth

Hospital (or other place) _____

Address _____

_____

Delivered by _____

Mother's Name

_____

First   Middle   Maiden   Married

Father's Name

_____

First   Middle   Last

Religion and Rites

Religion

Parents' Religious Affiliation(s) _____

_____

Local Congregation(s) Attended _____

_____

Rites
(Baptism, Circumcision, First Communion, Confirmation, Bar/Bat Mitzvah, Quinceañera Mass, Ordination, etc.)

Rite _____

_____

Date   Place   Officiant

_____

Witnesses, Godparents, or Other Special Participants

Rite _____

_____

Date   Place   Officiant

_____

Witnesses, Godparents, or Other Special Participants

Rite _____

_____

Date   Place   Officiant

_____

Witnesses, Godparents, or Other Special Participants

Rite _____

_____

Date   Place   Officiant

_____

Witnesses, Godparents, or Other Special Participants

My Siblings

Name _____

_____

Birth Date   Birthplace

Shared Parents   ☐ Mother   If not, mother's name _____

                   ☐ Father   If not, father's name _____

Name _____

_____

Birth Date   Birthplace

Shared Parents   ☐ Mother   If not, mother's name _____

                   ☐ Father   If not, father's name _____

Name _____

_____

Birth Date   Birthplace

Shared Parents   ☐ Mother   If not, mother's name _____

                   ☐ Father   If not, father's name _____

Name _____

_____

Birth Date   Birthplace

Shared Parents   ☐ Mother   If not, mother's name _____

                   ☐ Father   If not, father's name _____

Name _____

_____

Birth Date   Birthplace

Shared Parents   ☐ Mother   If not, mother's name _____

                   ☐ Father   If not, father's name _____

Education/Professional Development

School Name   Location   Years Attended

School Name   Location   Years Attended

School Name   Location   Years Attended

School Name   Location   Years Attended

School Name   Location   Years Attended

School Name   Location   Years Attended

School Name   Location   Years Attended

Degree   Granting Institution   Date Granted

Degree   Granting Institution   Date Granted

Degree   Granting Institution   Date Granted

Degree   Granting Institution   Date Granted

Professional License/Certification   Granting Organization   Date

Professional License/Certification   Granting Organization   Date

Professional License/Certification   Granting Organization   Date

Professional License/Certification   Granting Organization   Date

Marriages/Partners

Name of Spouse/Partner (include all former surnames) _____
_____

Date of Ceremony and Place _____

If Ended, Date and How _____

Name of Spouse/Partner (include all former surnames) _____
_____

Date of Ceremony and Place _____

If Ended, Date and How _____

Name of Spouse/Partner (include all former surnames) _____
_____

Date of Ceremony and Place _____

If Ended, Date and How _____

Name of Spouse/Partner (include all former surnames) _____
_____

Date of Ceremony and Place _____

If Ended, Date and How _____

Name of Spouse/Partner (include all former surnames) _____
_____

Date of Ceremony and Place _____

If Ended, Date and How _____

My Children

Name _____

Birth Date, Birthplace _____

Relationship (Natural, Adoption, Foster-, Step-, etc.) _____

Child's Other Parent(s) _____

Name _____

Birth Date, Birthplace _____

Relationship (Natural, Adoption, Foster-, Step-, etc.) _____

Child's Other Parent(s) _____

Name _____

Birth Date, Birthplace _____

Relationship (Natural, Adoption, Foster-, Step-, etc.) _____

Child's Other Parent(s) _____

Name _____

Birth Date, Birthplace _____

Relationship (Natural, Adoption, Foster-, Step-, etc.) _____

Child's Other Parent(s) _____

Name _____

Birth Date, Birthplace _____

Relationship (Natural, Adoption, Foster-, Step-, etc.) _____

Child's Other Parent(s) _____

Name _____

Birth Date, Birthplace _____

Relationship (Natural, Adoption, Foster-, Step-, etc.) _____

Child's Other Parent(s) _____

Residences

Fill in all your residences since birth, or earliest known.

Full Address _____

Co-Owner(s)/Occupants_____

Rented/Owned? _____

Dates of Residence _____

Full Address _____

Co-Owner(s)/Occupants_____

Rented/Owned? _____

Dates of Residence _____

Full Address _____

Co-Owner(s)/Occupants_____

Rented/Owned? _____

Dates of Residence _____

Full Address _____

Co-Owner(s)/Occupants_____

Rented/Owned? _____

Dates of Residence _____

Full Address _____

Co-Owner(s)/Occupants_____

Rented/Owned? _____

Dates of Residence _____

Residences

Fill in all your residences since birth, or earliest known.

Full Address _____

Co-Owner(s)/Occupants_____

Rented/Owned? _____

Dates of Residence _____

Full Address _____

Co-Owner(s)/Occupants_____

Rented/Owned? _____

Dates of Residence _____

Full Address _____

Co-Owner(s)/Occupants_____

Rented/Owned? _____

Dates of Residence _____

Full Address _____

Co-Owner(s)/Occupants_____

Rented/Owned? _____

Dates of Residence _____

Full Address _____

Co-Owner(s)/Occupants_____

Rented/Owned? _____

Dates of Residence _____

Employment

Do not include military service.

Job Title _____

Company _____

Address _____

Start/End Dates _____

Job Title _____

Company _____

Address _____

Start/End Dates _____

Job Title _____

Company _____

Address _____

Start/End Dates _____

Job Title _____

Company _____

Address _____

Start/End Dates _____

Job Title _____

Company _____

Address _____

Start/End Dates _____

Memberships

These include civic, social, school/alumni, service, historical/genealogical, religious, or other organizations.

Organization (include chapter) _____

Place and Years _____

Position(s) Held _____

Organization (include chapter) _____

Place and Years _____

Position(s) Held _____

Organization (include chapter) _____

Place and Years _____

Position(s) Held _____

Organization (include chapter) _____

Place and Years _____

Position(s) Held _____

Organization (include chapter) _____

Place and Years _____

Position(s) Held _____

Organization (include chapter) _____

Place and Years _____

Position(s) Held _____

Organization (include chapter) _____

Place and Years _____

Position(s) Held _____

Military Service

Branch of Service   Enlistment Date   Discharge Date

Billet (Job Rating/Training)	Postings (Locations)	Unit	Dates Served

Military Service

Awards and Rank Advancements

Title	Date	Description

3

stories about early family life

This chapter helps you write about your parents and siblings and the roles they have played in your life. It helps you gather their memories of themselves and your shared family life, too. Try to document basic statistics (birth, marriage, and death information) for each and every family member, whether or not you are part of each others' lives today. Then add as many details about lives, personalities, and relationships as you wish.

When writing about family, you may experience the pleasures of reliving meaningful moments and rich relationships that perhaps you haven't recalled recently. Savor the process of remembering the best times with your loved ones. These memories can enrich your present (and future, through this book) as much as they enriched your past. Describe them with whatever details come to mind: stories, composite memories, or explanations of how someone made you feel special.

Several of the pages on your parents and siblings are designed to be filled out by them, if possible. You can certainly fill out these pages yourself, but think how valuable it will be to collect your loved ones' descriptions of themselves! The data requested on individual family members (birth, marriage, etc.) may be more accurate if your loved ones fill them out themselves. Certainly capturing their own perspectives—and even their own handwriting—is worth the effort of sending them these pages.

If you need (or prefer) to fill out this information without their assistance, just do your best. If you are grieving the loss of a loved one or the end of a relationship, you may choose to leave that person's description aside for the present. Consider at least writing the basic statistics and (in pencil) a brief statement like, "I can't write about this now without being sad [or angry]." You can say more when you are ready. If you have a strained relationship with a parent or sibling, see chapter 1 for more advice on writing about difficult subjects. If you really don't want to write your unpleasant feelings, consider giving a short, neutral description based on facts such as, "My sister was tall and good at math." And if this section will stop you in your tracks from recording your life story, then skip it for now and move on to the stories you want to tell.

tips

» If your parents and/or siblings have passed away and you are lacking information, contact someone who might know: a spouse, child, or another relative.

» Use About My Mother and About My Father forms to honor all who have shared those roles in your life, whether natural, adoptive, foster-, or step-parents. Do the same thing with your siblings (natural, step-, etc). Distinguish between multiple mothers or fathers with an explanatory note at the top of the page (e.g., "this is my father's first wife").

» A page doesn't have to be complete in order to include it. Perhaps you know next to nothing about a birth parent, or your parents did not marry or stay together. Consider acknowledging that much on the appropriate form and moving on.

About My Mother

Name

_____

First   Middle   Maiden   Married

_____

Birth Date   (Day, Month, Year)

_____

Birthplace

_____

Death Date   Burial Location

> **HINT**
>
> Insert a copy of her birth or infant baptismal certificate or other mementoes related to information on this page. You may fill out additional copies of maternal information forms for step-mothers, birth/ adoptive mothers, etc.

Her Mother _____

Full Name _____

Race/Ethnicity/Nationality _____

Birth Date, Birthplace _____

Death Date, Location _____

Her Father _____

Full Name _____

Race/Ethnicity/Nationality _____

Birth Date, Birthplace _____

Death Date, Location _____

Raised by (if Not Parents):

_____

Names   Relation

About My Mother

_____

Where Raised _____

_____

Place(s) and Dates

_____

Place(s) and Dates

Siblings

Name _____

Birth Date, Birthplace _____

Spouse _____

Death Date, Place _____

Name _____

Birth Date, Birthplace _____

Spouse _____

Death Date, Place _____

Name _____

Birth Date, Birthplace _____

Spouse _____

Death Date, Place _____

Name _____

Birth Date, Birthplace _____

Spouse _____

Death Date, Place _____

About My Mother

Religion

Her Family's Religious Denomination _____

Name of Congregation _____

Education

School Name	Place	Years Attended
School Name	Place	Years Attended
School Name	Place	Years Attended
School Name	Place	Years Attended
School Name	Place	Years Attended
School Name	Place	Years Attended

Residences (not including places lived with my father)

Address	Years	Description
Address	Years	Description
Address	Years	Description
Address	Years	Description
Address	Years	Description
Address	Years	Description

About My Mother

Additional Marriages (not including marriage to my father)

Name of Spouse/Partner (include all former surnames) _____
_____

Date of Ceremony and Place _____

If Ended, Date and How _____

Name of Spouse/Partner (include all former surnames) _____
_____

Date of Ceremony and Place _____

If Ended, Date and How _____

Name of Spouse/Partner (include all former surnames) _____
_____

Date of Ceremony and Place _____

If Ended, Date and How _____

Name of Spouse/Partner (include all former surnames) _____
_____

Date of Ceremony and Place _____

If Ended, Date and How _____

Name of Spouse/Partner (include all former surnames) _____
_____

Date of Ceremony and Place _____

If Ended, Date and How _____

My Mother's Childhood Stories

AS REMEMBERED BY _____

Who was she named after? How does she feel about her name?

_____

_____

_____

_____

HINT

Insert photos of your mother at different ages. Looking at these pictures together can give you greater perspective about your mother's life.

What was she like as a child? Describe her appearance and personality. _____

_____

_____

_____

_____

_____

Describe her childhood home(s) and neighborhood(s). Tell about any place in her home, yard, or neighborhood that was special to her. _____

_____

_____

_____

_____

_____

Describe her upbringing: how she was raised, her financial circumstances, family health issues, or other significant things that shaped her as a person. _____

_____

_____

_____

_____

_____

My Mother: During My Childhood

_____

Complete this form if your mother was alive during your childhood. If your mother is still living, have her complete this form about herself, if possible.

What was your mother's daily life like while you were growing up? (Think about her employment, parenting, volunteering, recreation, travel, etc.) _____

_____

_____

Describe her health during these years (well-being, illnesses, injuries). _____

_____

_____

What were her greatest challenges during these years? _____

_____

_____

What were her triumphs or successes during these years? _____

_____

_____

What were her most rewarding relationships during these years? Her most difficult ones? _____

_____

_____

What were your mother's greatest goals or hopes during these years? Were they realized? _____

_____

_____

_____

Me & My Mother: Childhood

Describe the time you spent with your mother during your childhood.

What did you do together? Did you enjoy it? Did you spend enough
time together? _____

_____

_____

_____

_____

_____

_____

_____

_____

_____

_____

How did your mother show she cared about you? _____

_____

_____

_____

_____

_____

_____

_____

_____

_____

_____

_____

> **HINT**
>
> Send a copy of the companion form, Me & My Child, to your mother to fill out. Send Special Forms for her to document additional recollections.

Me & My Mother: Childhood

How did your mother discipline you? What did you think about her discipline methods then? What do you think now? _____

_____

_____

_____

_____

_____

_____

_____

How did your mother's opinions or beliefs (religious, cultural, social, political, etc.) affect you as a child?

_____

_____

_____

_____

_____

_____

_____

_____

Write any favorite memories of you and your mother during your childhood. _____

_____

_____

_____

_____

_____

_____

_____

About My Father

_____

Name

_____
First   Middle   Maiden   Married

_____
Birth Date   (Day, Month, Year)

_____
Birthplace

_____
Death Date   Burial Location

HINT

Insert a copy of your father's birth or infant baptismal certificate or other mementoes related to this page. You may fill out additional copies of paternal information forms for stepfathers, birth/adoptive fathers, etc.

His Mother _____

Full Name _____

Race/Ethnicity/Nationality _____

Birth Date, Birthplace _____

Death Date, Location _____

His Father _____

Full Name _____

Race/Ethnicity/Nationality _____

Birth Date, Birthplace _____

Death Date, Location _____

Raised by (if Not Parents):

_____
Names   Relation

About My Father

Where Raised _____

_____

Place(s) and Dates

_____

Place(s) and Dates

Siblings

Name _____

Birth Date, Birthplace _____

Spouse _____

Death Date, Place _____

Name _____

Birth Date, Birthplace _____

Spouse _____

Death Date, Place _____

Name _____

Birth Date, Birthplace _____

Spouse _____

Death Date, Place _____

Name _____

Birth Date, Birthplace _____

Spouse _____

Death Date, Place _____

About My Father

Religion

His Family's Religious Denomination _____

Name of Congregation _____

Education

School Name	Place	Years Attended
School Name	Place	Years Attended
School Name	Place	Years Attended
School Name	Place	Years Attended
School Name	Place	Years Attended
School Name	Place	Years Attended

Residences (not including places lived with my mother)

Address	Years	Description
Address	Years	Description
Address	Years	Description
Address	Years	Description
Address	Years	Description
Address	Years	Description

About My Father

Additional Marriages (not including marriage to my mother)

Name of Spouse/Partner (include all former surnames) _____

_____

Date of Ceremony and Place _____

If Ended, Date and How _____

Name of Spouse/Partner (include all former surnames) _____

_____

Date of Ceremony and Place _____

If Ended, Date and How _____

Name of Spouse/Partner (include all former surnames) _____

_____

Date of Ceremony and Place _____

If Ended, Date and How _____

Name of Spouse/Partner (include all former surnames) _____

_____

Date of Ceremony and Place _____

If Ended, Date and How _____

Name of Spouse/Partner (include all former surnames) _____

_____

Date of Ceremony and Place _____

If Ended, Date and How _____

My Father's Childhood Stories

_____ _____

Who was he named after? How does he feel about his name?

_____

_____

_____

_____

> ### HINT
> Insert photos of your father at different ages. Looking at these pictures together can give you greater perspective about your father's life.

What was he like as a child? Describe his appearance and personality. _____

_____

_____

_____

_____

_____

Describe his childhood home(s) and neighborhood(s). Tell about any place in his home, yard, or neighborhood that was special to him. _____

_____

_____

_____

_____

_____

Describe his upbringing: how he was raised, his financial circumstances, family health issues, or other significant things that shaped him as a person. _____

_____

_____

_____

_____

_____

My Father: During My Childhood

Complete this form if your father was alive during your childhood. If your father is still living, have him complete this form about himself, if possible.

What was your father's daily life like while you were growing up? (Think about his employment, parenting, volunteering, recreation, travel, etc.) _____

_____

_____

Describe his health during these years (well-being, illnesses, injuries). _____

_____

_____

What were his greatest challenges during these years?_____

_____

_____

What were his triumphs or successes during these years? _____

_____

_____

What were his most rewarding relationships during these years? His most difficult ones?_____

_____

_____

What were your father's greatest goals or hopes during these years? Were they realized? _____

_____

_____

_____

Me & My Father: Childhood

AS REMEMBERED BY _____

Describe the time you spent with your father during your childhood.

What did you do together? Did you enjoy it? Did you spend enough
time together? _____

_____

_____

_____

_____

_____

_____

_____

_____

_____

_____

How did your father show he cared about you? _____

_____

_____

_____

_____

_____

_____

_____

_____

_____

_____

_____

> **HINT**
>
> Send a copy of the
> companion form, Me &
> My Child, to your father
> to fill out. Send Special
> Forms for him to document
> additional recollections.

Me & My Father: Childhood

AS REMEMBERED BY

How did your father discipline you? What did you think about his discipline methods then? What do you think now? _____

_____

_____

_____

_____

_____

_____

_____

How did your father's opinions or beliefs (religious, cultural, social, political, etc.) affect you as a child?

_____

_____

_____

_____

_____

_____

_____

Write any favorite memories of yourself and your father during your childhood. _____

_____

_____

_____

_____

_____

_____

_____

My Parents' Relationship

_____

HINT

Include a photo of your parents together and/or a copy of their marriage certificate or announcement on a Memorabilia page.

If possible, have one (or both) of your parents fill out this section about themselves. Fill out additional copies for step-parents, etc.

How did your parents meet? Describe their dating life. _____

_____

_____

_____

_____

_____

_____

_____

Marriage

_____

Date   Place

What was their wedding (or early time together) like? _____

_____

_____

_____

_____

Residences My Parents Shared

_____

Place   Years   Description

_____

Place   Years   Description

_____

Place   Years   Description

My Parents' Relationship

AS REMEMBERED BY _____

What was their relationship like? What interests and values did they share? How were they different? How did

they work out conflicts? _____

_____

_____

_____

_____

_____

_____

_____

_____

_____

What did you learn from their relationship? (If a parent is filling this out: What did you learn from your rela-

tionship that you want your child to know?) _____

_____

_____

_____

_____

_____

_____

_____

_____

_____

If the relationship ended:

_____

Date   Circumstance (Death, Divorce, Legal Separation, etc.)

About My Sibling

HINT

Insert photos of your sibling at different ages.

Have each sibling complete a copy of this form, or complete it on their behalf.

Name

_____

First   Middle   Last

_____

Gender

_____

Birth Date, Birthplace

_____

Death Date   Burial Location

Parents We Share

☐ Mother (if Not, Mother's Name: _____)

☐ Father (if Not, Father's Name: _____)

Raised by (if Not Parents):

_____

Names   Relation

Education

_____

School Name   Place   Years Attended

_____

School Name   Place   Years Attended

_____

School Name   Place   Years Attended

_____

School Name   Place   Years Attended

_____

School Name   Place   Years Attended

About My Sibling

Marriages

Name of Spouse/Partner (include all former surnames) _____

_____

Date of Ceremony, Place _____

If Ended, How and When _____

Name of Spouse/Partner (include all former surnames) _____

_____

Date of Ceremony, Place _____

If Ended, How and When _____

Children

Name _____

Birth Date, Birthplace _____

Spouse _____

Death Date_____

Name _____

Birth Date, Birthplace _____

Spouse _____

Death Date_____

Name _____

Birth Date, Birthplace _____

Spouse _____

Death Date_____

My Sibling's Childhood Stories

_____

Have each sibling complete a copy of this form, or complete it on their behalf.

Who were you named after? How do you feel about your name? _____

_____

_____

_____

_____

_____

_____

_____

_____

_____

What were you like as a child? Describe your appearance and personality as you remember them.

_____

_____

_____

_____

_____

_____

_____

_____

_____

_____

Me & My Sibling During Childhood

AS REMEMBERED BY _____

Send a copy of this form to each of your siblings, and fill it out yourself about each of them.

What was your relationship like with your sibling? Did one lead/follow, tease, bully, ignore, and/or look out for the other? Were you rivals and/or friends? _____

_____

_____

_____

_____

What did you and your sibling share: bedroom, toys, clothes, books, or the lime light? How well did you share these? _____

_____

_____

_____

_____

Write something unique about your relationship: a special language or joke you shared, common interests, intense rivalry, etc. _____

_____

_____

_____

_____

Write any additional memories of you and your sibling. _____

_____

_____

_____

_____

4

stories from childhood

Our earliest years shaped our lives and often include our fondest memories. But the older we get, the more remote our youngest years can seem. The task of transforming wispy or forgotten childhood recollections into vivid, written ones can seem daunting. This chapter will help, with a steady stream of carefully targeted questions and plenty of flexibility for your memories to flow in whatever direction they may.

Many people don't have clear, consistent memories of life before age ten, but most of us do remember something. We may recall that we were generally happy. We may have sensory memories that manifest when we smell mothballs (Grandma's closet) or eat frozen custard (summers at the beach). We may have composite memories of playing in a backyard or neighborhood park over the course of many years. It is also common to have vivid memories of highly emotional or stressful childhood events: a parent's departure, surgery, the state spelling bee competition.

When you start to think about your childhood, those recollections may surface first and overshadow other memories. You may need to prod yourself to look past those prominent memories to recall the details and events of everyday life. After all, a typical childhood is constructed of daily routines, not action-packed drama.

Finally, our childhood memories may not always make sense. When we stored young memories away, they were relatively raw—perhaps just images, emotional impressions, or song fragments. We didn't assign the same complex meanings to them that we would today.

To reconstruct your earliest memories, use the same process you use to reconstruct other memories: Lay out what you remember, elaborate on it to the best of your ability, and ask others for help. You can rely on any of the memory-jogging techniques mentioned in chapter 1. Alternatively, borrow memories from parents, siblings, or your gossipy longtime neighbor. You have to do this, to some extent. After all, you don't recall your own birth and infancy. You have likely already adopted other people's memories as your own without being aware of it. You can also borrow memories from photographs or home movies, which often offer important clues to events and personalities. When you are aware that a memory is borrowed, try to credit the source.

You can also research your own past, as it's possible to research almost any topic online. With Google Maps **<maps.google.com>**, you can virtually retrace the walk from your apartment to the elementary school or use the Street View function to see an image of the apartment or school (if they are still there). Look for stats on your high-school state basketball championship game. Research a family member's illness, religious or ethnic background, or another topic that affected your life when you were too young to understand the details. Again, credit the information you find and try to connect it to a personal recollection: "*According to the state athletics association website*, we won the championship game by a wide margin (84–55), but all I really remember is the long ride to the game with my girlfriends, and screaming ourselves hoarse in the stands."

My Birth

_____

Additional details about your birth are requested in chapter 2.

_____

Birth Date   (Day, Month, Year)

_____

Birthplace

HINT

Send a parent or older sibling a request for stories about your infant and toddler years. If your parent kept a baby book for you, look for answers there.

What were the circumstances of your parents' lives before your birth or adoption? _____

_____

_____

_____

_____

_____

_____

_____

_____

What have you been told about your birth (including who was there or who should have been, labor or delivery complications, your appearance or health at birth, your parents' feelings)? _____

_____

_____

_____

_____

_____

_____

_____

_____

_____

_____

My Birth

Why were you named as you were? How did you feel about your name when you were young? What about now? _____

_____

_____

_____

_____

_____

What do you know about your early health and physical development (teething, talking, walking, eating, and social behavior)? _____

_____

_____

_____

_____

_____

Write down stories you have been told about yourself as a baby or toddler, including those about your relationships with siblings, parents, or others. _____

_____

_____

_____

_____

_____

_____

_____

_____

_____

_____

Childhood Personality

_____

Describe your personality as a child: shy, friendly, outgoing, nervous, energetic, obedient, willful, funny, charming, competitive. Share any memories that show your personality. _____

_____

_____

_____

_____

_____

_____

_____

_____

_____

_____

_____

_____

_____

> **HINT**
>
> Just for fun, send copies of this form to your parent(s) and/or sibling(s) to fill out about you. See how your memories and opinions are similar and different.

Who influenced your tastes and interests most during your childhood? _____

_____

_____

_____

_____

_____

_____

_____

_____

Childhood Personality

AS REMEMBERED BY _____

What did you really like to do as a child (crafts, games, electronics, art, building or inventing things, music, visiting museums, sports, writing, playing outside, being with friends)? _____

_____

_____

_____

_____

_____

_____

_____

_____

_____

_____

_____

_____

_____

_____

_____

_____

_____

_____

_____

_____

_____

_____

_____

Home

Address

HINT

Include photos of your home or neighborhood.

When did you live here? _____

_____

Describe your home. Think about the layout, size, décor, comfort level, and special details or rooms you liked or disliked. _____

_____

_____

_____

_____

_____

_____

_____

_____

Describe any improvements you and/or your family made to your home or yard. What difference did these improvements make? _____

_____

_____

_____

_____

_____

_____

_____

_____

_____

_____

Home

Where did you spend most of your time when you were at home? What did you do there? _____

_____

_____

_____

_____

_____

_____

Write about your yard and/or neighborhood. Was it busy, peaceful, loud, dangerous, grassy, friendly, fun, huge, or boring? _____

_____

_____

_____

_____

_____

_____

_____

_____

Who did you interact with in your neighborhood? _____

_____

_____

_____

_____

_____

_____

_____

_____

Everyday Life

Before you started school, who took care of you? Who else was with you? What kinds of things did you do? Share a memory (even a fragment or a borrowed memory) from your preschool years. _____

_____

_____

_____

_____

As a school-age child, what was your after-school routine like? Who took care of you? _____

_____

_____

_____

_____

_____

What did you do on weekends or other days off? Who was with you? _____

_____

_____

_____

_____

_____

_____

What did you do during the summer? Who took care of you? _____

_____

_____

_____

_____

_____

_____

Everyday Life

Did you like to be at home? Why or why not? _____

_____

_____

_____

_____

What kinds of foods did your family eat? Describe mealtimes, favorite foods, who prepared meals, etc. What

were your favorite (and least favorite) foods? _____

_____

_____

_____

_____

What kinds of chores did you do? Did you help take care of siblings or other youngsters? _____

_____

_____

_____

_____

_____

Was your home clean, cluttered, or chaotic? Who took charge of neatness? _____

_____

_____

_____

_____

_____

_____

Everyday Life

For what were you punished as a child, and how were you punished? _____
_____
_____
_____
_____
_____

What did you do for fun at home? Whom did you play with? Share a playtime memory. _____
_____
_____
_____
_____
_____

Describe any favorite toys. Why did you love them? Share a memory about toys. _____
_____
_____
_____
_____
_____

What television shows or radio programs did your family enjoy? Did you have a favorite? _____
_____
_____
_____
_____
_____

Everyday Life

What did you read for fun when you were young? Did anyone read with you?_____

_____

_____

_____

_____

_____

Did you go to the movies or the theater as a child? Share memories of a favorite show or a fun time out.

_____

_____

_____

_____

_____

What did you wear most days and on special occasions? Describe any clothes you loved or hated.

_____

_____

_____

_____

_____

_____

Describe pets your family had. How did you feel about them? Who took care of them? _____

_____

_____

_____

_____

_____

My Childhood Health

Describe any medical conditions you had when you were born. What measures were taken to correct or manage those conditions? _____

_____

_____

_____

_____

_____

_____

HINT

If you don't know these answers, ask someone. Attach a copy of your immunization record, an allergy or hospital ID bracelet, or other evidence of your physical health and well-being in your younger years.

_____

_____

_____

_____

_____

Were you immunized?   ☐ Yes   ☐ No   ☐ Not Sure

Were you breast-fed?   ☐ Yes   ☐ No   ☐ Not Sure

Were you colicky?   ☐ Yes   ☐ No   ☐ Not Sure

Describe what you know of your health as an infant and toddler. Include things like allergies, frequent ear infections or colds, asthma, or delays in normal physical development (like walking and talking). _____

_____

_____

_____

_____

_____

_____

_____

My Childhood Health

AS REMEMBERED BY _____

What about your health during your elementary- and middle-school years? Did you have any broken bones or teeth, surgery, or physical or speech therapy? Did you wear glasses or braces? Write any memories of being physically able-bodied or restricted. _____

_____

_____

_____

_____

_____

_____

_____

_____

_____

_____

_____

_____

_____

_____

_____

_____

_____

_____

_____

_____

_____

_____

_____

Childhood Companions

Describe your earliest childhood playmates and friends from school. What were they like? What did you do together? _____

_____

_____

_____

_____

_____

HINT

Include a Special People form for particularly close friends. Send Special Memories forms to childhood friends, or use them yourself to describe a particularly memorable experience with a friend.

_____

_____

_____

_____

_____

_____

Tell about any childhood "enemies": a bully; an athletic, academic, or social rival; or a grown-up or kid who just seemed to have it in for you. _____

_____

_____

_____

_____

_____

_____

_____

_____

_____

_____

Childhood Companions

Write about time spent with family friends (your parents' friends). What kinds of things did you all do together? What other children were there? Did you enjoy this time?_____

_____

_____

_____

_____

_____

_____

_____

_____

_____

_____

_____

_____

_____

_____

_____

_____

_____

_____

_____

_____

_____

_____

_____

_____

_____

_____

Elementary School Days

For names and locations of schools attended, see chapter 2.

What is your earliest memory of elementary school? _____

_____

_____

_____

_____

Write about any traditions you and your family observed at the beginning of the school year. _____

_____

_____

_____

_____

List any elementary teachers you recall. What do you remember about them? _____

_____

_____

_____

_____

How did you feel about school? In what subjects did you perform well? Poorly? _____

_____

_____

_____

Describe a time when you were teased by or embarrassed in front of your peers. How did you react? What do you think about that now? _____

_____

_____

_____

Elementary School Days

What did you eat for lunch at school? Describe your lunchtime. _____

_____

_____

_____

What were your favorite activities during recess?_____

_____

_____

_____

Describe any special elementary school activities or honors: student of the month, orchestra, school play, crossing guard, teacher's helper, spelling bee, math competition, or a compliment from a teacher.

_____

_____

_____

Did you ever get in trouble, or were you sent to the principal's office? What for? _____

_____

_____

_____

Think about activities you did outside of school: Scouts, 4-H, music lessons, karate class, etc. Write memories of your participation (age, name of organization, leaders or friends, and what your participation meant to you).

_____

_____

_____

_____

_____

Middle Grades

For names and locations of schools attended, see chapter 2.

How did your school life change when you reached middle or junior high school? _____

_____

_____

Describe your social life and friendships during junior high school. _____

_____

_____

Describe a time when you were teased or embarrassed in front of your peers. How did you react? What do
you think about that experience now? _____

_____

_____

List any middle-grade teachers you recall. Describe any memories of them. _____

_____

_____

How did you feel about going to school each day? How well did you do in different subjects? _____

_____

_____

Tell about any extra activities you were involved with during these years (sports, clubs, etc.) What did it mean
to you to be involved in these? _____

_____

_____

_____

_____

Middle Grades

Describe any special honors or compliments you recall receiving during junior high or middle school years. What did you think of these at the time? _____

_____

_____

_____

_____

Write about a disappointment you recall in school: doing unexpectedly poorly on a test or project, losing a student election, not placing in a competition, etc. How do you feel about that experience now?

_____

_____

_____

_____

Did you ever get in trouble? What for? _____

_____

_____

How do you feel now about your overall experience in middle or junior high school? _____

_____

_____

_____

What did you do during school vacations in the spring, summer, and winter (as well as any other breaks you had)? _____

_____

_____

_____

_____

Childhood Celebrations & Traditions

How did your family celebrate your birthday when you were young? Were there parties? Who came? What were your favorite gifts? Was your birthday ever a disappointment? _____

_____

_____

_____

_____

How did your family (or your parents, if you weren't invited) celebrate the New Year when you were a child? Write about the first time you recall staying up until midnight. _____

_____

_____

_____

_____

What holidays or traditions did your family observe during the spring? _____

_____

_____

_____

_____

Write your memories of national or patriotic celebrations. Where did you celebrate, how, and with whom? How did you feel about them? _____

_____

_____

_____

_____

_____

_____

_____

Childhood Celebrations & Traditions

How did your family celebrate Halloween? Tell about any favorite costumes, parties, decorations, food, where you trick-or-treated, haunted house tours, etc. _____

_____

_____

_____

_____

How did you celebrate Thanksgiving or other fall celebrations? Where did you gather? Who cooked and baked? Write about the tastes, smells, and other sensory memories. _____

_____

_____

_____

_____

What winter holidays did your family celebrate? Write about a typical holiday observance. decorations, music, food, gift-giving, religious rituals, and family traditions. _____

_____

_____

_____

_____

What additional holidays did your family observe? Describe your traditions. _____

_____

_____

_____

_____

_____

_____

5

stories from high school

Whether you came of age in the 1940s or 1990s, your teen years were likely full of "firsts": first job, first date, first time behind the wheel. You made decisions about college, career, perhaps even marriage and childbearing. However, you may still have kept one foot in childhood, refusing to surrender beloved toys or rituals even as you started shaving.

Your high school years are likely a mixed bag of memories. You may recall some poignant coming-of-age tales; power struggles with your parents; and made-for-movie moments in which you scored gloriously (on or off the field). You've also probably got memories of everyday life in which you went to school, faced down finals, and hoped you'd have something exciting to do on Friday night. As with childhood memories, dramatic memories may overshadow everyday ones.

In this chapter, you will record both. The memory prompts will hit the highlights and also the stories and relationships of everyday life. And while some people are wary of facing their teenage selves—with memories of social awkwardness, bad decisions, or long-buried pain over things that went wrong—you will also look at the positives: your friendships, kindnesses, and good choices. Record your current feelings about past experiences whenever you can. Today's perspective is part of the process of telling your story. Anything you learned, any sense of humor or compassion you show toward your younger self—these are valuable both to yourself and to your readers.

Researching your teen years is way more fun than it sounds. If you left a paper trail of any kind—letters or notes, diaries, yearbooks—read them. You may find yourself charmed by your sense of humor, or feeling a new compassion for this young kid who was just trying to navigate high school halls without mishap. In yearbook entries, you may find evidence of friendships, hopeless crushes, inside jokes, and other social drama long forgotten.

Indulge yourself in the sights, sounds, and scenes of the past. Listen to old Top-40 albums. Try on your old letter jacket. Tour a vintage car show. Attend a high school football game. Watch a defining movie of that age, whether it was *Rebel Without a Cause*, *The Graduate,* or *The Breakfast Club*. Jog your memories of fads and fashions by flipping through lifestyle magazines from your teen years, *Remember That?* (Family Tree Books) or the *This Fabulous Century* series (Time-Life Books).

Relationships are especially crucial for this section of your life. Connecting with others, such as old friends, can spark a lot of memories and offer opportunities for others to participate in your book. Get in touch with a high school buddy, teacher, or coach. The folks at home still influenced you too, even if you spent most of your time at school, work, friends' houses, or the alley behind the five-and-dime. You'll also write about your relationships with your parents and siblings. You can give credit where it is due—with a family member who worked hard to care for you—and/or explain family challenges you faced at a young age.

Teenage Personality

_____

How would you describe your personality as a teenager? How did you act
around others your age, when with family, and at school? _____

_____

_____

_____

_____

HINT

Just for fun, send copies of
this form to your parent(s)
and/or sibling(s) to fill out
about you. See how your
memories and opinions are
similar and different.

How did you respond to new challenges or situations? _____

_____

_____

_____

_____

What did you think of yourself at this age? Were you confident, critical, or accepting of yourself? What do you
think about your teenage self now? _____

_____

_____

_____

_____

What did you like to do on your own: daydream, read, listen to the radio, watch television, work on hobbies or
collections, play sports, or wander your neighborhood? _____

_____

_____

_____

_____

_____

Teenage Personality

AS REMEMBERED BY _____

What were you good at as a teenager? Think about all kinds of gifts, talents, or interests: social, musical, athletic, artistic, leadership, academic, inventive, compassionate, etc. _____

_____

_____

_____

_____

What did you believe about right and wrong, religion, and the like? Whose values, opinions, or actions influenced your beliefs most during these years? _____

_____

_____

_____

_____

_____

_____

_____

Tell about a time (or more than one time) when you were kind to someone or did a good deed. _____

_____

_____

_____

Tell about a time when you were mean or unkind to someone. _____

_____

_____

_____

_____

Health and Well-Being

How healthy were you as a teenager? How did your health or any injuries affect your daily life at home, at school, and with friends? _____

_____

_____

_____

_____

_____

_____

_____

_____

HINT

If you don't know the answers for this page, ask someone. Attach a Memorabilia page with a copy of a doctor's chart, hospital ID bracelet, or related mementoes.

Think about your physical growth and changes as a teenager: acne, being the tallest or shortest, "getting your figure," etc. How did these changes affect you? _____

_____

_____

_____

_____

_____

Describe your emotional health as a teenager: Were you happy, anxious, nervous, depressed, angry, aggressive, low-key, content, moody? How did you and your family handle any emotional difficulties you experienced? _____

_____

_____

_____

_____

_____

_____

Tough Teenage Choices

Feel free to skip this form if you prefer not to answer these questions—or add a blank continuation page and tell lots of stories!

What were common attitudes among your friends toward teenage drinking, smoking, drug use, or reckless or illegal behavior?_____

_____

_____

_____

_____

_____

How did your parents feel about these activities? What motivations did they give you for avoiding them?

_____

_____

_____

_____

_____

Write about your choices regarding teenage drinking, smoking, drug use, or reckless or illegal behavior. What motivated you? What were your experiences like? What consequences did you face? What impact did your choices have on your life?_____

_____

_____

_____

_____

_____

_____

_____

_____

_____

Planning for the Future

As a teen, how did you feel about the future: excited or afraid? Or did you ignore the future altogether?

_____

_____

_____

_____

_____

_____

_____

What did you want to do when you grew up? How passionate were you about your plans? _____

_____

_____

_____

_____

_____

_____

_____

How did your plans for the future shape the choices you made in high school? _____

_____

_____

_____

_____

_____

_____

_____

_____

Planning for the Future

How did your circumstances as a teen affect your hopes for the future? Consider things like money, access to education, romantic ties, and obligations to loved ones. _____

_____

_____

_____

_____

_____

_____

_____

_____

How did others' attitudes affect your hopes for the future? Did your parents have strong feelings about what they wanted you to do? _____

_____

_____

_____

_____

_____

_____

_____

What did you want to do when you finished high school—and what did you actually do? Why? What do you think of those choices today? _____

_____

_____

_____

_____

_____

Home Life

What were your responsibilities at home during your teen years? Describe any chores you had. Did you do your own cooking, laundry, tidying, etc.? _____

_____

_____

_____

_____

_____

_____

_____

_____

Did you receive an allowance or spending money? If so, did you have to earn it, and what did you do with it? How did this affect you, both then and now?_____

_____

_____

_____

_____

_____

_____

_____

Describe your home environment during your teenage years: peaceful, (un)comfortable, (un)predictable, (un)happy, (in)tolerant, (un)welcoming, or boring? Did you enjoy being at home? Did your friends like to come over?

_____

_____

_____

_____

_____

_____

_____

_____

Home Life

How did your parents treat you when you were a teenager? Were they interested in your thoughts and feelings? How did they discipline you? How much did they trust you? _____

_____

_____

_____

_____

_____

_____

_____

If you had siblings, did your parents treat you and your siblings pretty much the same, or were there differences? How did you feel about this at the time? What do you think about it now? _____

_____

_____

_____

_____

_____

_____

_____

Looking back, how do you think your home life influenced your decisions and friendships as a teenager?

_____

_____

_____

_____

_____

_____

_____

_____

Me & My Mother: Teen Years

AS REMEMBERED BY _____

Describe your relationship with your mother during your teen years. What did you do together? _____

_____

_____

_____

_____

_____

_____

_____

_____

_____

_____

_____

HINT

Fill out another copy for a step-mom. Send the companion form Me & My Teenager to your mother to fill out about you. Send her Special Memories forms to request additional recollections.

What did you agree or disagree about? How did you work out conflict? _____

_____

_____

_____

_____

_____

_____

_____

_____

_____

_____

_____

_____

_____

Me & My Mother: Teen Years

AS REMEMBERED BY _____

How did your mother support you during these years? Consider employment, sacrifices made, time spent together, help with homework, listening, offering advice, etc. If your mother was not supportive, write about that. _____

_____

_____

_____

_____

_____

_____

_____

_____

_____

_____

_____

_____

_____

Write any special memories of you and your mother from your teen years. _____

_____

_____

_____

_____

_____

_____

_____

_____

_____

Me & My Father: Teen Years

_____

Describe your relationship with your father during your teen years. What did you do together? _____

_____

_____

_____

_____

_____

_____

_____

_____

_____

_____

_____

HINT

Fill out another copy for a step-dad. Send the companion form Me & My Teenager to your father to fill out about you. Send him Special Memories forms to request additional recollections.

What did you agree or disagree about? How did you work out conflict? _____

_____

_____

_____

_____

_____

_____

_____

_____

_____

_____

_____

_____

Me & My Father: Teen Years

AS REMEMBERED BY _____

How did your father support you during these years? Consider employment, sacrifices made, time spent together, help with homework, listening, offering advice, etc. If your father was not supportive, write about that.

_____
_____
_____
_____
_____
_____
_____
_____
_____
_____
_____
_____

Write any special memories of you and your father from your teen years. _____

_____
_____
_____
_____
_____
_____
_____
_____
_____
_____
_____
_____

Me & My Sibling: Teen Years

_____

_____
Sibling's Name

How would you describe your relationship with your sibling during your teen years? _____

_____

_____

_____

_____

_____

_____

What kinds of things did you do together? What did you talk about? _____

_____

_____

_____

_____

_____

_____

_____

What interests or attitudes did you and your siblings share? _____

_____

_____

_____

_____

_____

Me & My Sibling: Teen Years

AS REMEMBERED BY _____

What did you disagree or fight about? How did you work out conflict?_____

_____

_____

_____

_____

_____

_____

_____

Tell about a time your sibling showed you special attention, love, or consideration, and/or a time you did that

for him or her._____

_____

_____

_____

_____

_____

_____

_____

_____

Write about any more special memories of you and your sibling during your teen years. _____

_____

_____

_____

_____

_____

_____

_____

High School Days

For names and locations of schools attended, see chapter 2.

Describe your high school campus and the student body: size, social/ethnic backgrounds, values, educational ambitions. How did you fit in? _____

_____

_____

_____

_____

List any memorable high school teachers, counselors, or coaches. What made them memorable? How did they treat or influence you? _____

_____

_____

_____

How did you feel about going to school each day? How did you do academically? _____

_____

_____

_____

_____

Were you ever recognized for special talents or achievements? How? Did you receive compliments, awards, honors, or leadership or other opportunities? _____

_____

_____

_____

_____

High School Days

Write about a time when you were disappointed in your performance (as a student, athlete, or in another area). How do you feel about that experience now? _____

_____

_____

_____

_____

Did you ever get in trouble at school? What for? _____

_____

_____

_____

_____

If you graduated, write about your high school graduation. If you didn't graduate, write about why not, or what you were doing instead. _____

_____

_____

_____

_____

_____

What did you do during school vacations in the spring, summer, and winter (as well as any other breaks you had)? _____

_____

_____

_____

_____

_____

Friends

Who were your closest friends when you were a teenager? Describe them. How did you get to be friends? What did you do together? How did you feel about them? _____

_____

_____

_____

_____

HINT

Fill out a Special People form for close friends. Use a Special Memories page to describe a particularly memorable experience with a friend. Send Special Memories forms to friends from high school to request their thoughts of your time together.

Write about your larger circle of friends, if you had one. What did you have in common? How loyal were you to each other? _____

_____

_____

_____

_____

Did you ever argue or fight with a good friend? Who? What happened? How did it end? _____

_____

_____

_____

_____

Where did you hang out with friends? A restaurant, shopping center, park, or other location? Why? Describe it.

_____

_____

_____

_____

_____

_____

Friends

Who were your rivals at school, on the sports field, or in your social life? Write about your conflicts and how they went._____

_____

_____

_____

_____

Did you ever take any social risks, like befriending a less-popular kid, standing up for an unpopular cause, or treating a popular kid badly? Tell what happened. Was it worth it? _____

_____

_____

_____

_____

Tell about a time you were teased or embarrassed in front of your peers. How did you react? What do you think about that now?_____

_____

_____

_____

_____

In what way(s) did you stand out from the crowd as a teenager: looks, abilities, race, religion, personal interests, gender, attitudes, or culture? How did this affect your social life and your sense of yourself? _____

_____

_____

_____

_____

_____

Romance

Describe any school or community dances you attended. Did you enjoy them? Who did you dance with? What kind of music or dancing was there? What did you wear? Don't forget Homecoming, prom, or Sadie Hawkins (girls' choice) dances. _____

_____

_____

_____

_____

_____

_____

_____

_____

_____

HINT

Use Special People forms to write about significant romantic relationships. Attach copies of love notes, dance cards, prom photos, snapshots of boy/girlfriends, etc. If you're feeling brave, send Special Memories pages to old boy/girlfriends to fill out.

Tell about your first romance or crush. What attracted you? How did the relationship go?_____

_____

_____

_____

_____

_____

_____

_____

_____

_____

_____

_____

_____

Romance

How interested were you in dating, and what was your dating life like? Name any serious boy/girlfriends, and describe your relationship(s). _____

_____

_____

_____

_____

_____

_____

How did you learn about "the birds and the bees"? _____

_____

_____

_____

_____

_____

_____

_____

Share any thoughts on teenage romance. What lessons did you learn about love (and/or sexuality) during your teenage years? What advice would you give young people today on this topic? _____

_____

_____

_____

_____

_____

_____

_____

Fashions

What were clothing fashions like when you were a teenager? Think about colors, shoes/boots, and accessories like jewelry, hats, scarves, and sunglasses. Who were famous fashion icons at the time? _____

_____

_____

_____

_____

HINT

Look through old photos and your yearbooks to remind yourself of high school fashions. The beginning of this chapter lists other resources that can remind you about fads and fashions. Add Memorabilia pages with images of the fads and fashions you write about.

How did you typically dress during your teenage years? Did you like the way you dressed? Why did you dress this way?_____

_____

_____

_____

_____

Describe a favorite outfit. _____

_____

_____

_____

_____

How did you style your hair as a teenager? How did this style compare to those of your peers? Did you like your hairstyle? _____

_____

_____

_____

_____

_____

_____

Fads

What kind of music was popular during your teen years? What did you think
of it? _____
_____
_____

HINT

See the resources
referenced at the beginning
of this chapter for more
on fads and fashions. Add
Memorabilia pages with
images of the fads and
fashions you write about.

What music did *you* listen to as a teenager? Who influenced your tastes? Write
a memory connected to popular music. _____
_____
_____
_____
_____

What books, magazines, television shows, and movies do you recall from your teen years? Which were popular among your friends? Did any strongly influence the way you thought or acted?_____
_____
_____

Who were the popular heroes and celebrities of your teen years? Who were your favorites? Any teen idol
crushes or favorite females? _____
_____
_____

Write any sayings or phrases that were popular during your teenage years. (Think how you described something great—as "groovy" or "the bee's knees"—or an attractive person—"hot mama" or "babe.") _____
_____
_____
_____
_____
_____

Extracurricular Activities

What extracurricular activities did you do at school: sports teams, clubs, organizations, ensembles, social groups, productions, etc.? _____

_____

_____

_____

_____

_____

_____

_____

HINT

Attach team photos, newspaper clippings, or programs to Memorabilia pages.

What activities, clubs, or sports did you participate in outside of school: community, church, social, or service groups, teams, programs, or activities? _____

_____

_____

_____

_____

_____

_____

_____

Why did you participate in these activities? _____

_____

_____

_____

_____

_____

_____

Extracurricular Activities

Describe your experience with these activities. If it was competitive, how often did you practice? How long was the season? Did your team have a winning record? If it was a club, how often did you meet? What did you do? _____

_____

_____

_____

_____

_____

_____

_____

_____

What did you learn from participating in these activities? _____

_____

_____

_____

_____

_____

_____

_____

Describe a time you really shined during an extracurricular activity. _____

_____

_____

_____

_____

_____

_____

_____

First Job

What was your first paying job? Who did you work for? What did you do? _____

_____

_____

_____

_____

_____

_____

How old were you when you started this job? _____

_____

How much were you paid? _____

How did you get the job? _____

_____

_____

_____

Why did you work? _____

_____

_____

_____

_____

_____

_____

_____

First Job

How did you feel on your first day? _____

_____

_____

_____

_____

_____

_____

What did you learn by working? _____

_____

_____

_____

_____

_____

_____

_____

What did you do with the money you earned? _____

_____

_____

_____

_____

Why did you stop doing this job? _____

_____

_____

_____

_____

Behind the Wheel

HINT

Attach a photo
of your first car.

Who taught you how to drive? Describe any difficulties, fears, or mishaps
that happened. If you never learned to drive, explain why. _____

_____

_____

_____

_____

_____

_____

_____

How old were you when you got your driver's license, and how did you feel when you got it? _____

_____

_____

_____

_____

_____

_____

_____

_____

Did you have a car? If so, how did you get it? Describe any cars you drove—make, model, year, color, and
distinctive features, including any nickname you gave it. _____

_____

_____

_____

_____

_____

_____

_____

Behind the Wheel

How often did you drive, and where did you drive to? If you didn't drive, how did you get from place to place?

_____
_____
_____
_____
_____
_____
_____
_____
_____
_____
_____

What was your dream car as a teenager? Did anyone you knew have a great car? If so, describe it._____
_____
_____
_____
_____
_____
_____
_____
_____
_____
_____
_____
_____
_____
_____

6

stories from my professional life

"What do you do?" It's the first question many people in the United States ask when they meet someone socially. Why? Because "what you do," why you do it, and how you feel about it tell a lot about your character, values, interests, skills or talents, family or social culture, and endurance. This applies whether or not you have a high-paying job. In fact, sometimes, it's those with lower-paying (or nonpaying) work whose jobs reveal the most or the best about them.

For the purposes of this chapter, your "work" might include any combination of advanced education, paid employment, unpaid work around the house, military commitments, or volunteer service. You'll capture the different aspects of your daily work from young adulthood to retirement.

You will likely find yourself rearranging or skipping a section or two in this chapter; after all, most people haven't done everything! (If you have, congratulations! You have a lot to write about.) But you might find yourself adding things, too.

In this professional life chapter, questions about relationships revolve around people you have known as college buddies, coworkers, professors, bosses, fellow volunteers, etc. (Romance and family relationships are covered separately, in chapter 8.) The exception will be questions about how your professional life (and that of your partner) affected your personal and family life over the years. If your professional and personal life have been intertwined (your true love worked in the next cubicle over, or you were part of a family business), consider adding extra forms to describe how that worked out.

There is a special section called "Work in the Home" that focuses on the unpaid work of managing a household. It can be surprisingly satisfying to describe the work you've done at home, which is often underappreciated. Even if you were never the primary "homemaker" in your home, you likely shared responsibility for some chores, and you deserve a chance to document it. If your daily work included caring for children and/or a partner, you will have the opportunity to write more about that in chapter 7, Stories About a Family of Your Own.

You may have to dig deep into your memory to recall details about early employment, college years, and the like. Consider writing to former employers to request copies of your personnel files. Give yourself plenty of time to reminisce both alone and with others who can help you remember. Be patient: It's worth the effort, particularly to your readers, who want to know about your formative young-adult years. The decisions you made during that time and the lessons you learned are some of the most important you can pass along.

College

What colleges, technical schools, etc., did you apply to? Why did you apply there? _____

_____

_____

_____

_____

_____

_____

_____

_____

_____

_____

_____

HINT

Find more details in chapter 1 about schools attended. If you attended multiple colleges (including military academies), you may want to print additional College forms.

Where did you attend school? How did you feel about going there? _____

_____

_____

_____

_____

_____

_____

_____

_____

_____

_____

_____

_____

College

What did your family think about you going to school? Was it expected? Was anyone particularly proud, jealous, excited, angry, or sad about you going? _____

_____

_____

_____

_____

_____

_____

What concerns did your parents express about you going to school: money, grades, homesickness, social life, etc.? How did they show their concern?_____

_____

_____

_____

_____

_____

_____

What concerned you the most about going to college: money, grades, homesickness, social life, etc?

_____

_____

_____

_____

_____

_____

_____

Academic Life

What course of study did you choose and why? Tell if you changed your major(s), and why. _____

_____

_____

_____

_____

_____

_____

_____

_____

_____

How well did you do in school overall? What classes did you most enjoy? Least enjoy? Did you attend classes

regularly, or skip them?_____

_____

_____

_____

_____

_____

_____

Describe your study habits. Did you study a lot or a little? Alone or with a group? _____

_____

_____

_____

_____

_____

_____

Academic Life

Think of a time you worked especially hard on a class assignment. What was it? How did it go? _____

_____

_____

_____

_____

_____

_____

_____

_____

Think of a time you ignored an important assignment or waited until the last minute. What were the results?

_____

_____

_____

_____

_____

_____

_____

_____

Write about a professor, tutor, or another mentor who made a difference in your college life. _____

_____

_____

_____

_____

_____

_____

_____

Campus Life

Describe your school campus: size, location, urban/rural, etc. Was there a spot on campus you particularly liked or avoided? _____

_____

_____

_____

_____

_____

HINT

Complete this form even if you commuted to class, or were a nontraditional student because you were older, married, or part-time.

Did you pledge a sorority or fraternity? Why or why not? _____

_____

_____

_____

_____

Where did you live while you were at school? What was it like? What did you eat? _____

_____

_____

_____

_____

Who did you live with at school? How did this person (or people) influence your experience? _____

_____

_____

_____

_____

_____

_____

Campus Life

What did you do—or where did you go—when you needed a break from campus life? Describe a favorite memory of a getaway. _____

_____

_____

_____

_____

_____

_____

_____

_____

If you lived at home (or visited during school breaks), how did your relationship with your parents/siblings change? Did you still have to obey "house rules" about curfews, chores, etc.? How did you feel about that?

_____

_____

_____

_____

_____

_____

What was your school vacation schedule? What did you usually do during breaks? _____

_____

_____

_____

_____

_____

_____

_____

Extracurricular Activities

What extracurricular activities did you participate in while in college? Describe sports teams (intramural or through your school), clubs, organizations, ensembles, social groups, productions, etc. _____

_____

_____

_____

_____

_____

_____

_____

_____

_____

Why did you participate in these activities? _____

_____

_____

_____

_____

_____

_____

Describe your experience with these activities. If it was competitive, how often did you practice? How long was the season? Did your team have a winning record? If it was a club, how often did you meet? What did you do? _____

_____

_____

_____

_____

_____

_____

Extracurricular Activities

What role, if any, did political or cultural activism play in your daily life and/or major decisions during your college years? _____

_____

_____

_____

_____

_____

_____

_____

_____

_____

_____

_____

What role, if any, did religion play in your daily life and/or major decisions during your college years? _____

_____

_____

_____

_____

_____

_____

_____

_____

_____

_____

_____

_____

Social Life

Who were your best friends at school? How did you meet? What did you like about each other? _____

_____

_____

_____

_____

_____

Was there a particular group of friends you associated with, like those who participated in arts, sports, Greek life, or those with shared culture, race, or politics? _____

_____

_____

_____

_____

_____

What were your biggest social pressures as a student? How did you handle them? _____

_____

_____

_____

_____

_____

Describe a time or place you felt very alone or out of your comfort zone. _____

_____

_____

_____

_____

_____

Graduation

Describe your college graduation. If you did not graduate, write about why not or what you were doing instead. _____

_____

_____

HINT

Add a Memorabilia page with a copy of your diploma and/or graduation photos.

_____

_____

_____

_____

_____

_____

What did you want to do right after college—and what did you actually do? Why? What do you think of those choices today? _____

_____

_____

_____

_____

_____

_____

_____

Did you ever go back to school (attend graduate school, continuing education, etc)? Why or why not? _____

_____

_____

_____

_____

_____

_____

_____

Work Life

Describe your first full-time job. How old were you when you started? How long did it take you to find a full-time job?_____

_____

_____

_____

_____

_____

_____

_____

What were your hopes and expectations for your working life? Did you plan to make a lot of money quickly, grow in a career path over time, or stay at the same job until retirement?_____

_____

_____

_____

_____

_____

_____

How did you feel during your first six months to a year of full-time work? What did you learn about yourself and about your job? _____

_____

_____

_____

_____

_____

_____

_____

Work Life

If you switched jobs a lot, how did you feel about that? Did you like these changes or were they hard on you? Why? _____

_____

_____

_____

_____

_____

_____

_____

If you have not yet retired, what are your goals or hopes for your future career? _____

_____

_____

_____

_____

_____

_____

If you have not yet retired, what are your concerns about your future career? _____

_____

_____

_____

_____

_____

_____

_____

_____

Jobs

HINT

Print as many of these forms as you need to cover your full paid work history.

_____
Employer Name

_____
Employer Location

_____
Date(s) Employed

_____
How much were you paid?

_____
What was your schedule (hours per week)?

Why did you want this job? _____

_____

_____

How did you get this job? (How did you find out about it? Who helped or recommended you? What was your interview like? How did you feel when you got it?) _____

_____

_____

_____

_____

What skills, techniques, or knowledge did you have to learn on the job in order to succeed? Who taught you?

_____

_____

_____

_____

_____

_____

_____

Jobs

How well did you do at this job? Think about your skills, productivity, working well with others, following orders or instructions, etc. _____

_____

_____

_____

_____

_____

Why did you stop working here? How did you feel about leaving? _____

_____

_____

_____

_____

What life lessons did you learn at this job? What about other benefits, like friends made or skills learned?

_____

_____

_____

_____

_____

What effect, if any, did this job have on your personal or family life? _____

_____

_____

_____

_____

_____

_____

Work in the Home

This section captures the unpaid work of managing a household. These questions apply to most everyone, whether you were a "homemaker" or not.

Who managed your household during your adult life? If it changed over the years, how did it change? _____

_____

_____

What were your household duties (cooking, cleaning, clothing care, shopping, gardening/yard work, preserving food, caring for livestock or pets, household repairs, auto maintenance, taking out the trash, arranging for repairs, etc.)? _____

_____

_____

If others lived in your home, what household chores did they do? _____

_____

_____

How did you feel about your household responsibilities? If there was a division of labor between you and a partner, how did you feel about that division? _____

_____

_____

Write about something you did around the house that you were proud of. Did you remodel or decorate? Fix or organize something? _____

_____

_____

_____

_____

_____

Work in the Home

For what labor-saving household devices have you been most grateful? Why? _____

_____

_____

What chores do you like the least? _____

_____

_____

What chores do you enjoy, or what chores don't bother you so much? _____

_____

_____

Describe how you managed household finances (your role/your partner's role, how you kept track of expenses, how spending decisions were made). How well did you manage your finances? _____

_____

_____

Looking back, what did you do well in handling your household responsibilities? _____

_____

_____

_____

What do you wish you'd done better in your household responsibilities? _____

_____

_____

_____

_____

Retirement

Why did you retire when you did? _____

_____

_____

_____

How did you feel about retiring? _____

_____

_____

_____

How was your retirement celebrated or honored (by yourself or others)?_____

_____

_____

_____

What did you do immediately after you retired?_____

_____

_____

_____

How well did you adjust to retirement? How long did it take you to adjust? _____

_____

_____

If you had a partner at the time you retired, how did your partner feel about your retirement? What changes, if

any, occurred in your relationship? _____

_____

_____

_____

Retirement

How did your financial health change after retirement? What adjustments, if any, did you make to your life-style?_____

_____

_____

What changes, if any, did you have in friends when you retired? Did you make new ones or spend more time with those you already had? _____

_____

_____

If you returned to paid employment after you officially retired, why?_____

_____

_____

What activities have you enjoyed since retiring that you didn't do (or do as much) when you were working?

_____

_____

Today, what do you enjoy about being retired? _____

_____

_____

What do you miss about working, if anything? _____

_____

_____

_____

_____

_____

_____

Military

For more details about military service, see chapter 2. Consider writing about combat or other intense military experiences on a Life-Changing Experience form.

How did you decide to join the military, or were you drafted? What were you feeling when you joined?

_____

_____

What did your parents and/or other loved ones think about you joining the military? _____

_____

_____

_____

How did you decide which branch of the military to join? _____

_____

_____

Describe your experience as a trainee (boot camp, ROTC, etc). What did you think of it? (If you attended a military academy, describe this experience in the College and Academic Life forms earlier in this section?

_____

_____

_____

Who were your friends during your military service? Why did you get along? _____

_____

_____

_____

_____

_____

_____

Military

What did you think of your commanding officer(s)? _____

_____

_____

Write about where you were stationed. What did you like or dislike about the base(s) or location(s)? _____

_____

_____

_____

_____

_____

What were your daily job responsibilities? What did you think of them? _____

_____

_____

_____

What did you do when you were off duty? _____

_____

_____

_____

How did active duty affect your family and/or romantic relationships? Who did you miss the most? Who missed you? _____

_____

_____

_____

_____

_____

Military

Write about a time you were commended for your work. _____
_____
_____

Write about a time you were disciplined, if you ever were. _____
_____
_____
_____
_____
_____

Were you ever deployed? How did you feel about being deployed or not being deployed? _____
_____
_____
_____

If you were deployed, describe your assignment(s). What did you do during this time? _____
_____
_____
_____

What security clearance did you have, if any? What did you think of having (or not having) clearance? _____
_____
_____
_____
_____
_____
_____

Military

Write about a time you were in harm's way, if you ever were. What happened? Where were you? How did that experience change you? (Consider writing about combat on a Life-Changing Experiences form.)

_____

_____

How did others treat you as a soldier, officer, or nurse, etc? Do you feel you were treated differently in the military because of your gender, race, religion, etc.?_____

_____

_____

Think of someone you admired or respected during your time in the military: an officer, soldier, political figure, relative, etc. Why did you admire that person? _____

_____

_____

How did you feel when you completed your military service? _____

_____

_____

What lessons did you learn from serving in the military?_____

_____

_____

How do you feel today about the country, ideals, or people you served?_____

_____

_____

_____

_____

_____

Volunteer

HINT

For immersion volunteer experiences like the Peace Corps or traveling missionary service, consider filling out Special Memories or Life-Changing Experience forms.

_____
Name of Organization

_____
Branch/Location

_____
Dates of Service

_____
Position(s) Held

Why did you volunteer here? _____

_____

_____

_____

_____

What type of service did you perform? Describe the amount of time, the type of work, etc. _____

_____

_____

_____

_____

Write about a time that volunteering was hard or you had to give more than you expected. What was the result? _____

_____

_____

_____

_____

_____

_____

_____

Volunteer

Describe someone you met through volunteering whom you came to respect or admire. What did you admire about or learn from that person?_____

_____

_____

_____

_____

_____

Write about a time you had fun or otherwise enjoyed your volunteer work. _____

_____

_____

_____

_____

_____

How did volunteering change you? What rewards did you feel personally from it? _____

_____

_____

_____

_____

_____

Why did you stop volunteering, if you stopped? _____

_____

_____

_____

_____

_____

stories about a family of my own

In this chapter you will write about the family life you've lived in adulthood. Here you can celebrate your closest family relationships. You might write about the moment you realized how much your partner loved you, those late nights cuddling your newborn son, or your joy in your daughter's (or granddaughter's) successes.

Don't skimp on this section. The people most likely to read this book are your own family members. Think how much it will mean to them to read that they have mattered in your life! Your sincere written appreciation, love, and shared memories can especially nurture vulnerable or rocky relationships, or those that have cooled over time. And what about those who are no longer part of your daily life because of a death, divorce, or another circumstance? Write about them as much as you are able or willing.

You may want to try some of the memory-jogging tricks in chapter 1 to bring more memories to life. If you find yourself unsure of what to write regarding a parent, sibling, etc., consider using your favorite pictures of them as a starting point. Write captions explaining why you love each picture. Does it capture something special about that person's character? Was it taken at an event you remember fondly? The process of thinking about the person may help you express what has been special about the individual or unique about your relationship.

You probably know plenty of embarrassing stories about your family, but think twice about telling them all. Similarly, where important family memories involve secrets, consider whether these are your secrets to share, or seek permission from someone who would be affected by your sharing them. Choose tactful and sensitive ways to share feelings or memories that might cause a loved one pain. Consider using the old rule of thumb to write five positive things about someone for every negative thought expressed.

You didn't live family life alone. Why would you want to record it alone? Enlist the help of your family for this chapter. Ask family members to fill out pages about themselves and their relationships with you, if possible. Having someone's description of herself and of her relationship with you is an important emotional artifact. You'll cherish those pages as a reminder of her and her interest in you. Where relationships have been less than healthy, consider writing the relationship pages yourself and expressing the way you wish things were.

tips

» Each "Partner" and "Child" section has multiple pages. If you and a partner or child didn't build a lasting relationship, you might skip pages that ask you to describe your relationship in detail. Wedding pages can be skipped if you were not married, or may be used to describe a commitment ceremony or similar event. If you had no children or romantic partner, you can skip those pages entirely.

» Create Special People pages for extended relatives who have played significant roles in your adult years.

» Missing information on a page is okay. A single entry on a form is valuable.

About My Partner

_____

Name

_____

First   Middle   Surname (Maiden/Previous Married)

_____

Birth Date   (Day, Month, Year)

_____

Birthplace

_____

Death Date   Burial Location

HINT

Insert a copy of your partner's birth or infant baptismal certificate or other mementoes relating to information requested on this page.

Mother _____

Full Name _____

Race/Ethnicity/Nationality _____

Birth Date, Birthplace _____

Death Date, Place _____

Father _____

Full Name _____

Race/Ethnicity/Nationality _____

Birth Date, Birthplace _____

Death Date, Place _____

Raised by (if Not Parents):

_____

Names   Relation

About My Partner

AS REMEMBERED BY _____

Where raised _____

_____

Place(s) and Dates

_____

Place(s) and Dates

Siblings

Name _____

Birth Date, Birthplace _____

Spouse _____

Death Date, Place _____

Name _____

Birth Date, Birthplace _____

Spouse _____

Death Date, Place _____

Name _____

Birth Date, Birthplace _____

Spouse _____

Death Date, Place _____

Religion

Family's Religious Denomination _____

Name of Congregation _____

About My Partner

Education

_____

High School   Place   Years Attended

_____

College   Place   Years Attended

Health (significant illnesses, medical conditions, injuries, etc.) _____

_____

_____

_____

_____

_____

Employment (including work in the home) _____

_____

_____

_____

_____

_____

Hobbies (including volunteer activities, handicrafts, sports and outdoor recreation, collections, etc.) _____

_____

_____

_____

_____

_____

_____

_____

_____

_____

About My Partner

Values and beliefs (including religious, civic, political, or other affiliations)_____

_____

_____

_____

_____

_____

_____

_____

_____

_____

_____

Additional Marriages/Romantic Partners (not including me)

Name of Spouse/Partner (include all former surnames) _____

_____

Date of Ceremony and Place _____

If Ended, Date and How _____

Name of Spouse/Partner (include all former surnames) _____

_____

Date of Ceremony and Place _____

If Ended, Date and How _____

Name of Spouse/Partner (include all former surnames) _____

_____

Date of Ceremony and Place _____

If Ended, Date and How _____

My Partner: Life Stories

AS REMEMBERED BY _____

What was your partner like as a child? Describe his or her appearance and

personality._____

_____

_____

_____

_____

_____

_____

> **HINT**
>
> Have your partner fill this out about himself/herself, if possible. If you are filling out pages for more than one partner, write your partner's name across the top of the page.

Describe your partner's childhood community or neighborhood(s). Was it friendly or impersonal, crowded or

isolated, urban or rural, safe or dangerous, rich or poor? Was everyone like your partner's family, or did your

family members stand out? _____

_____

_____

_____

_____

_____

Describe your partner's home(s). Did he or she like where he or she lived? Describe any place in his or her

home, yard, or neighborhood that was special to your partner._____

_____

_____

_____

_____

_____

_____

_____

_____

My Partner: Life Stories

What were your partner's teenage years like? You might describe your partner's high-school experiences, what he or she did with free time (work or play), and important friendships. _____

_____

_____

_____

_____

_____

_____

_____

_____

Describe your partner's young-adult years: college, work, travel, romance, starting a family. What were your partner's favorite decisions and his or her regrets? _____

_____

_____

_____

_____

_____

_____

_____

_____

What are your goals for the future? You might mention hopes and dreams about your career/retirement, family, finances, personal enrichment, or leisure time. _____

_____

_____

_____

_____

_____

Our Dating Life

_____

How did you two meet? _____

_____

_____

What attracted you to your partner? _____

_____

_____

What attracted your partner to you? _____

_____

_____

Describe your courtship or dating life. Mention special outings, funny moments, tender times. _____

_____

_____

When and how did you meet your partner's family? How did you feel? How did it go?_____

_____

_____

If you lived together while dating, when did you move in together? What led to your decision? Note memories about moving in together (or choosing not to). _____

_____

_____

_____

_____

_____

_____

Our Engagement

AS REMEMBERED BY _____

How did you decide to get married? Describe the proposal. _____

_____

_____

_____

If you formalized your engagement with a ring, write your memories about it. (Describe the ring, picking it out,

what made it special, etc.) _____

_____

_____

What was your engagement like? Long or short? Did you spend a lot of time together? Live together or apart?

_____

_____

_____

How did you feel during your engagement? Tell about moments of joy or doubt, and any pressure from friends

or family._____

_____

_____

_____

What prewedding celebrations did you have? Describe an engagement party, bridal shower, bachelor/ette

party, and/or rehearsal dinner. _____

_____

_____

_____

_____

Our Wedding

AS REMEMBERED BY _____

_____

Marriage Date _____ Place _____

Officiant _____ Title _____

Why we married there _____

_____

_____

HINT

Insert copies of wedding photos or marriage documents. If you fill out pages about more than one wedding, put your partner's name across the top of the page.

Attendants   Relationship to Bride/Groom

Best Man

_____

Matron/Maid of Honor

_____

Bridesmaid

_____

Bridesmaid

_____

Bridesmaid

_____

Bridesmaid

_____

Groomsman

_____

Groomsman

_____

Groomsman

_____

Groomsman

_____

Ring Bearer

_____

Flower Girl(s)

Our Wedding

AS REMEMBERED BY _____

Describe the wedding ceremony. Include details that are important to you about the location or setting, clothing (dresses/tuxedos), the program, your rings, the important participants, etc. _____

_____

_____

_____

_____

_____

_____

Describe the reception or other post-wedding celebration. Include details that are important to you about the location, decorations, flowers, food, cake, music, entertainment, etc. _____

_____

_____

_____

_____

_____

Describe your honeymoon. Where did you go, and why, and for how long? Recall tender or funny memories or mishaps. _____

_____

_____

_____

_____

_____

_____

_____

Newlyweds

_____

Think of your early time together, after your initial courtship/marriage. This might be your first year of marriage, the time period after moving in together, etc.

How did you spend time together as newlyweds (or as a newly committed couple)? Think of work, play, sports, hobbies, dates, or just hanging out. _____

_____

_____

_____

_____

_____

How did you feel when you were together? Apart? _____

_____

_____

_____

_____

Write about a happy event or moment with your partner during this time. _____

_____

_____

_____

_____

_____

What struggles did you have in your relationship? How did you handle them? _____

_____

_____

_____

_____

Newlyweds

What were your circumstances like at this time (financial, health, family issues, etc)? How did you handle
them? _____

_____

_____

_____

Write about an experience that made you grow closer as a couple. _____

_____

_____

_____

_____

Write about an experience that pulled you apart as a couple. How did you handle it?_____

_____

_____

_____

_____

What important lessons did you learn (yourself or as a couple) during this time?_____

_____

_____

_____

How did each of you change, adapt, or sacrifice during this time for the sake of your relationship? How do you
wish you or your partner had changed? _____

_____

_____

_____

Building a Life Together

AS REMEMBERED BY _____

Think of your time together after you settled in as a couple. This might be the time following your first year as a couple, or after you became parents, etc. (Parenting as a couple is addressed in another section.) If you fill out this form for more than one partner, write your partner's name across the top of the page.

When you got over the newness or novelty of being together, how did your feelings about your partner change or grow? _____

_____

_____

_____

_____

After you'd been together for a while, how did you spend your free time together? How important to you was spending time together?_____

_____

_____

_____

Write about a happy time with your partner during this time._____

_____

_____

_____

_____

What struggles did you have in your relationship? How did you handle them? _____

_____

_____

_____

_____

_____

Building a Life Together

AS REMEMBERED BY _____

What were your circumstances like at this time (financial, health, family issues, etc)? How did you handle them? _____

_____

_____

_____

Write about an experience that made you grow closer as a couple. _____

_____

_____

_____

Write about an experience that pulled you apart as a couple. How did you handle it? _____

_____

_____

_____

What important lessons did you learn (yourself or as a couple) during this time? _____

_____

_____

_____

How did each of you change, adapt, or sacrifice during this time for the sake of your relationship? How do you wish you or your partner had changed? _____

_____

_____

_____

_____

_____

My Partner Today

What do you love most about your partner right now? _____

_____

_____

HINT

Fill out this form if you have a living partner; have your partner fill out a copy about you, too.

_____

_____

What about your partner is challenging or difficult for you? _____

_____

_____

_____

_____

_____

When it's just the two of you at home, what is your partner like?_____

_____

_____

_____

_____

_____

What is your partner like in a public or social setting? What kinds of public or social settings does your partner enjoy (or avoid)? _____

_____

_____

_____

_____

_____

My Partner Today

AS REMEMBERED BY _____

Describe your partner's sense of humor. Give an example of something your partner would find funny or entertaining. _____

_____

_____

_____

What kinds of challenges does your partner handle well? What kinds of situations are difficult for your partner? _____

_____

_____

_____

How would you describe your partner's values or beliefs today? How have those beliefs grown or changed in your time together? _____

_____

_____

_____

What is an admirable quality or skill your partner has that you lack? _____

_____

_____

_____

What do you miss about your partner when you're not together? _____

_____

_____

_____

_____

Parenting With My Partner

_____

HINT

Fill out this page for any partner with whom you had a natural/adopted child (your partner could fill it out, too). If you were a solo parent, fill out the Solo Parenting form instead of (or in addition to) this one.

How did you feel when you learned you would be a parent? How did your partner feel?_____

_____

_____

Write about your experience as a couple during pregnancy or adoption. How did you handle your stresses and/or excitement? _____

_____

_____

_____

Describe a special or tender moment you shared as expectant or new parents. _____

_____

_____

What changed about your relationship when you became parents? How did you handle the changes?_____

_____

_____

How did your daily lives (work, leisure, etc.) change when you had children? How did you and your partner handle these changes? _____

_____

_____

_____

_____

_____

_____

_____

Parenting With My Partner

AS REMEMBERED BY _____

What did you do well as a new parent? What did your partner do well? What did you or your partner struggle with as new parents? _____

_____

_____

What parenting responsibilities did you share when your child(ren) was an infant? What about later? How did you feel about your division of parenting responsibilities? _____

_____

_____

Describe your parenting style compared to your partner's. How did these similarities or differences affect your relationship? Your child(ren)? _____

_____

_____

What changes or growth in yourself have you seen as a result of being a parent? _____

_____

_____

Who has been a source of support to you as parents? What kind of support have they offered? What difference has it made in your lives? _____

_____

_____

_____

_____

_____

_____

_____

About My Child

First   Middle   Last Name

Birth Date   (Day, Month, Year)

Place of Birth

Hospital (or Other Location)

Address

Delivered by

Other Parent's Name

Describe your memories of your child's birth. If you were not present, write what you know about your child's birth.

_____

_____

_____

_____

_____

_____

_____

_____

_____

_____

_____

_____

_____

_____

_____

About My Child

My Child's Education

_____

School Name   Place   Years Attended

_____

School Name   Place   Years Attended

_____

School Name   Place   Years Attended

_____

School Name   Place   Years Attended

Religion

Share memories of these events on Special Memories pages. Put copies of certificates, photos, etc. on Memorabilia pages.

Religious Affiliation(s):

_____

Rite   Date   Place   Officiant

_____

Witnesses, Godparents, or Other Special Participants

_____

Rite   Date   Place   Officiant

_____

Witnesses, Godparents, or Other Special Participants

_____

Rite   Date   Place   Officiant

_____

Witnesses, Godparents, or Other Special Participants

_____

Rite   Date   Place   Officiant

_____

Witnesses, Godparents, or Other Special Participants

Memories of My Child

_____

What did your child look like as a baby and/or young child? Mention any family
resemblances. _____

_____

_____

_____

_____

> **HINT**
> Insert copies of photos
> of your child at various
> ages, including photos
> with you and/or the child's
> other parent.

What was your child's personality like as a baby or toddler? You might describe mannerisms, social skills, and
likes or dislikes. _____

_____

_____

_____

_____

What did you enjoy most about your child when he or she was young? _____

_____

_____

_____

_____

_____

What was your child's health like as a baby or child (wellness, illnesses, injuries)? _____

_____

_____

_____

_____

_____

Memories of My Child

AS REMEMBERED BY _____

As your child grew, did he or she remind you of yourself or another loved one? In what ways? _____

_____

_____

How did your growing child show his or her independence? _____

_____

_____

_____

What did you admire most about your child during his/her teenage or young adult years? _____

_____

_____

Write about choices your teen or young adult made that were difficult for you. Why were they difficult? How

did they turn out? _____

_____

_____

_____

_____

Describe anything you wish you'd done differently while raising your child. _____

_____

_____

_____

_____

_____

_____

Everyday Life With My Children

AS REMEMBERED BY _____

When your children were young, what was your daily routine like? _____

_____

_____

_____

_____

When your children reached school age, what was the after-school routine like? _____

_____

_____

_____

_____

What did your family do on weekends or other days off? _____

_____

_____

_____

_____

What did your family do during the summers? (Document travel on a Travel Log or Special Memories form.)

_____

_____

What kinds of foods did your family eat? Describe mealtimes and favorite foods. Did one member of the family prepare special meals or desserts? _____

_____

_____

_____

_____

Everyday Life With My Children

Was your home clean, cluttered, or chaotic? Who took charge of neatness? _____
_____
_____

What chores did your children do? How did you motivate them to do their chores? _____
_____

What television shows, radio programs, or books did your family enjoy? _____
_____
_____

Did you take your children to the movies or the theater? Share memories of a favorite show or a fun time out.
_____
_____

Describe your family pets. Who took care of them? _____
_____
_____
_____

How did your professional life (and/or that of your partner) affect your family life? Would you do things differently if you could? _____
_____
_____
_____
_____
_____

My Grown-Up Child

Describe the path your child's life has taken since youth (education, work, family life, etc.). _____

_____

_____

_____

Describe his or her health during these years (well-being, illnesses, injuries).

_____

_____

_____

_____

What have been some of his or her challenges during these years?_____

_____

_____

_____

_____

What have been some of his or her successes during these years? _____

_____

_____

_____

What have been his or her most rewarding relationships during these years? The most difficult relationships?

_____

_____

_____

_____

_____

My Grown-Up Child

AS REMEMBERED BY _____

What are your child's favorite pastimes? _____

_____

_____

What are your child's goals or hopes for the future? (If he or she is not living, what were his or her goals or hopes in the last years of life, and were they realized?) _____

_____

_____

Marriages

Name (include all former surnames) _____

Date of Ceremony and Place _____

If Ended, Date and How _____

Name (include all former surnames) _____

Date of Ceremony and Place _____

If Ended, Date and How _____

Children

Name	Gender	Birth Date	Birthplace
Name	Gender	Birth Date	Birthplace
Name	Gender	Birth Date	Birthplace
Name	Gender	Birth Date	Birthplace
Name	Gender	Birth Date	Birthplace

About My Grandchild

Fill out this form for each grandchild and insert a copy behind his or her parent's form.

Full Name _____

Birth Date, Birthplace _____

Mother's Full Name (include maiden name) _____

Father's Full Name _____

Family's Religious Affiliation (if any) _____

Name of Congregation _____

Marriages

Name (include all former surnames) _____

Date of Ceremony and Place _____

If Ended, Date and How _____

Name (include all former surnames) _____

Date of Ceremony and Place _____

If Ended, Date and How _____

Children

Name	Gender	Birth Date	Birthplace
Name	Gender	Birth Date	Birthplace
Name	Gender	Birth Date	Birthplace
Name	Gender	Birth Date	Birthplace
Name	Gender	Birth Date	Birthplace

About My Grandchild

Write your memories and feelings about your grandchild's birth or adoption. _____
_____
_____

How would you describe your grandchild's personality and appearance? Does he or she remind you of other
family members? _____
_____
_____

What has your relationship with this grandchild been like throughout his or her life? How do you feel about
your relationship? _____
_____
_____

Write about any milestones in your grandchild's life (religious, cultural, educational, etc.). _____
_____
_____

What interests does your grandchild have? How are they reflected in his or her life? _____
_____
_____

What do you love most about your grandchild? _____
_____

What advice would you give your grandchild for now or the future? _____
_____
_____

reflections on my personal life and values

This chapter celebrates the person you are today, from your daily routines to your friendships. It helps you describe the unique space you have carved for yourself in this world. Topics include:

» **Memorabilia:** current photos of you

» **Daily Life:** the routines, rituals, places, and pastimes of your everyday life

» **My Home:** your current abode, be it dorm, apartment, condo, house, etc, along with its quirks and qualities

» **My Pet:** any furry, four-legged, or otherwise non-human, friends you have

» **Friendships:** who your best buddies are, what you do together, and your own role as a friend

» **My Hobbies:** whatever you like to create or do for fun

» **My Interests:** your favorite things

» **My Heritage:** your sense of your family legacy, your own personal traditions, and their meaning to you

» **My Values and Beliefs:** the standards, rules, or beliefs you live by, and why you live by them

» **My Hopes and Dreams:** what you want to accomplish or be, and what you wish you could be

» **My Legacy:** the memories you want to share with future generations

tips

» This chapter is all yours! You don't need to send pages to anyone else, because only your opinions and perspective are being asked for. Enjoy the luxury of having something be, unashamedly, all about you.

» Take your time while filling out this section. Don't rush your way through, or you'll leave an incomplete picture of what you're all about. Share your beliefs, as well as descriptions of the people, pets, and other things that make your life meaningful.

Memorabilia

Insert a current photo of yourself.

What do you like about your appearance now? _____

_____

_____

_____

_____

_____

_____

_____

_____

_____

_____

_____

What, if anything, do you wish were a little different? _____

_____

_____

_____

_____

_____

_____

_____

_____

_____

_____

_____

_____

_____

Daily Life

What's an average day like for you? What about your "days off"? _____

_____

_____

_____

_____

_____

What do you wear most days? What's your favorite outfit or piece of clothing? _____

_____

_____

_____

_____

_____

What are some of your habits or routines (e.g, morning coffee and paper, Sunday brunch, daily walks, can't miss TV show, mass every morning, Facebook every five minutes)? _____

_____

_____

_____

_____

_____

What do you do to unwind or relax?_____

_____

_____

_____

_____

_____

_____

Daily Life

What modern technologies or gadgets do you rely on in everyday life?_____
_____
_____
_____
_____
_____

Where do you go to eat out, or for drinks or dessert? How often do you go? Any restaurants you love for special occasions?_____
_____
_____
_____
_____
_____

How do you get where you're going—walk, ride, or drive? If you have a car, what's it like, and what do you think of it? _____
_____
_____
_____
_____
_____

When you have extra money to spend, what (and whom) do you spend it on? _____
_____
_____
_____
_____
_____

My Home

Address _____

_____

_____

Monthly rent or mortgage amount _____

Suggestion: If current, you may want to withhold this for security or privacy reasons.

HINT

Use a Special Places page to remember other places in which you've spent a lot of time, like a family cabin, cottage, condo, or annual vacation destination.

Move-in date: _____

Who lives with me: _____

_____

_____

_____

_____

_____

Describe your home (size, style, condition, layout). _____

_____

_____

_____

_____

_____

What's your favorite spot in your home? Why do you love it? _____

_____

_____

_____

_____

_____

My Home

Describe your neighborhood. _____

_____

_____

_____

_____

_____

How have you made the space your own (remodeling, decorating, landscaping, gardening, furniture, etc.)?

_____

_____

_____

_____

_____

What do you enjoy about your home? _____

_____

_____

_____

_____

_____

_____

What don't you like about your home? _____

_____

_____

_____

_____

_____

_____

My Pet

Use a page for each pet; place them here or in the appropriate section of your life (childhood, etc).

HINT

Place photos of your pet to record what your companion looks like.

_____
Name

_____
Birth Date or Approximate Age

_____
Adoption Date

_____
Breed   Gender

How did you get your pet? _____

_____

Describe your pet's physical appearance and personality. _____

_____

_____

How do you feel about your pet? _____

_____

_____

Who takes care of your pet? _____

_____

_____

What games or activities do you and your pet do together? _____

_____

_____

_____

My Pet

What are your pet's favorites (treats, toys, places, pastimes, people)? Least favorites? _____

_____

_____

_____

_____

_____

Where does your pet sleep? (Is this where you want your pet to sleep?) _____

_____

_____

_____

_____

_____

What adventures have you and your pet enjoyed together (travel, hikes, play dates, pet charity events)?

_____

_____

_____

_____

_____

Describe celebrations that include your pet (birthdays, holidays, annual photo portraits). _____

_____

_____

_____

_____

_____

_____

Friendships

Who would you say are your closest friends now? Why are you such good friends? What do you do together? _____

_____

_____

_____

_____

_____

HINT

Include friends' pictures or correspondence. Consider including a copy of a Special People page for each of your closest friends, past and present. Consider placing pages with past friends in the appropriate section (teen years, etc.).

Describe your larger circle of friends or acquaintances. Where do you see them? How often? What do you enjoy about these friends (or groups of friends)?

_____

_____

_____

_____

_____

Write about a friendship that is no longer part of your life that you miss. Who was this friend, and why was that person special to you? What happened, and how do you feel about it?_____

_____

_____

_____

_____

_____

_____

_____

_____

_____

_____

_____

Friendships

What kind of friend are you? What do you think your friends enjoy about you? What are your weaknesses as a friend? _____

_____

_____

_____

_____

_____

Describe memories of special occasions you have celebrating with friends. _____

_____

_____

_____

_____

_____

Write about a time a friend helped you in an important way. What did it mean to you? _____

_____

_____

_____

_____

Write about a time you helped out a friend, and what it meant to you (and/or that friend). _____

_____

_____

_____

_____

_____

_____

_____

My Hobbies

What activities have you enjoyed in your spare time throughout your life?_____

_____

_____

_____

_____

_____

What activities do you currently enjoy? How much time do you spend on them? _____

_____

_____

_____

_____

_____

What kinds of hobby equipment, tools, supplies, magazines/books, etc., do you own? Which have you used

the most? _____

_____

_____

_____

_____

_____

Describe something you have built or otherwise created. Are you proud of it?_____

_____

_____

_____

_____

_____

_____

My Interests

If someone hands you a newspaper, which section will you read first? Which won't you read at all? Why?
What kind of magazines do you enjoy? _____

_____

_____

What kinds of television shows and/or movies do you enjoy? _____

_____

_____

What kinds of events or attractions do you like to attend (exhibits, museums, fairs, charity events, community

dinners, races, festivals, concerts, etc.)? _____

_____

_____

What kind of music do you enjoy now? Favorite radio station? Band? Album? _____

_____

_____

What do you like to read? How much time do you spend reading? _____

_____

_____

What do you do for sports, outdoor recreation, or exercise (if you do these)? _____

_____

_____

What kinds of things do you not enjoy? _____

_____

_____

My Heritage

What values or principles did your parents, grandparents, or other relatives instill in you? In other words, what does your family name mean to you? _____

_____

_____

_____

_____

_____

_____

_____

_____

_____

_____

Describe family traditions you have continued to celebrate as an adult. Who participates? What do these traditions mean to you? _____

_____

_____

_____

_____

_____

_____

_____

_____

_____

_____

My Heritage

Describe traditions you have created yourself (or with a family of your own) as an adult. Who participates? What do these traditions mean to you? _____

_____

_____

_____

_____

_____

_____

As an adult, how have you observed birthdays with your loved ones? _____

_____

_____

_____

_____

_____

_____

_____

_____

As an adult, what food traditions have you created or passed on? Are there special foods or recipes among your loved ones now? Does one person do the cooking or baking? _____

_____

_____

_____

_____

_____

_____

_____

My Values & Beliefs

Describe your religious and/or philosophical beliefs. How have these changed over time?_____

_____

_____

_____

_____

Describe your political, social, and/or cultural views. How have these changed over time? _____

_____

_____

_____

_____

Who are your heroes? Why?_____

_____

_____

_____

_____

What is a cause or political/moral issue you have passionately supported? Why? _____

_____

_____

_____

_____

What is a political/moral issue or cause you have passionately opposed? Why? _____

_____

_____

_____

_____

My Values & Beliefs

What is a political/moral issue or cause that you feel conflicted or unsure about, or that you have changed your position on? Why? _____

_____

_____

_____

What would you say are the values that guide your life? _____

_____

_____

_____

Have your beliefs been dramatically influenced by one event, book, etc.? What was it? How did it change you?

_____

_____

_____

What causes, if any, do you support now (humanitarian, religious, environmental, political, social, animal rights, etc.)? How do you show your support? _____

_____

_____

_____

What do you consider a personality or character flaw about yourself that you wish you could change? Why?

_____

_____

_____

_____

_____

_____

My Hopes & Dreams

What is a goal you are actively working on now? Why do you want to achieve it? How confident are you of success? _____

_____

_____

_____

_____

What is a goal you would like to accomplish but haven't yet?_____

_____

_____

_____

_____

_____

What is a goal you wish you could accomplish but probably never will?_____

_____

_____

_____

_____

_____

What hopes and dreams do you have for your future?_____

_____

_____

_____

_____

_____

_____

My Hopes & Dreams

What would you do with all your time now if you were suddenly freed from your current obligations?

_____

_____

_____

_____

_____

_____

_____

_____

If you could choose your career or life's work all over again, what would you do? Why?_____

_____

_____

_____

_____

_____

_____

_____

_____

_____

If you could visit or live anywhere in the world for a time, where it would be, and why? _____

_____

_____

_____

_____

_____

_____

My Legacy

What do you hope people will remember about you? _____

_____

_____

_____

_____

_____

_____

_____

_____

_____

_____

_____

_____

_____

_____

_____

_____

_____

_____

_____

_____

_____

_____

_____

_____

_____

_____

_____

_____

My Legacy

What advice do you have for future generations?_____
_____
_____
_____
_____
_____
_____
_____
_____
_____
_____
_____
_____
_____
_____
_____
_____
_____
_____
_____
_____
_____
_____
_____
_____
_____
_____
_____
_____
_____

9

preserving your memories

Completing this book has helped you preserve your memories for both yourself and future generations. Now what about the physical artifacts of your life?

The "stuff of life" is also precious and worth preserving. Your treasures might be shoeboxes full of photos and memorabilia. Or it might be a vintage wedding gown, jewelry, or artwork. Most households have important papers that deserve preservation, too: recipes, letters, birth certificates, news clippings about family members, etc. How can you organize, identify, preserve, and share these?

Plan What to Keep

The first question to ask yourself is, "What do I have?" People can be surprised by what's lurking in bottom drawers, attics, and basements. Take a thorough tour of your home's nooks and crannies. Look for anything you've kept for sentimental or historical value. Your grandparents' marriage certificate and your mother's hope chest are obvious examples. But also look for items that will *become* heirlooms if you care for them properly, like your favorite childhood book or the birth announcement samplers your mother-in-law cross-stitched for each of your children. Don't overlook heirlooms hiding in plain sight: the quilt on your guest bed that Grandma made, or your great-grandmother's butterfly pin in the back of your jewelry box. Make a quick mental or physical inventory of your findings.

Next, consider carefully what's worth keeping indefinitely. You may be thinking *What?!? Shouldn't I keep* *every item of sentimental value?* The answer is no. As you read through this chapter and learn more about properly preserving your treasures, you'll find that many require pricey archival containers and/or particular storage conditions. When you see the preservation cost, you may be less willing to keep four hundred photos of your mother's cats. Or you may quickly realize that the only truly heirloom-friendly storage space in your home is a shelf or two in a shallow closet.

So how do you identify which family treasures are most precious to you? Well, if you were moving across the world tomorrow and could only take one sentimental object, what it would be? A close relative's personal belongings are often at the top of the list, imbued as they are with emotional memories. And which heirlooms are not as important to your legacy? These would be the items with no personal connection to yourself, like the wireless radio set you rescued from your neighbor's estate sale or large numbers of mass-produced trinkets. Also consider items that won't be as meaningful to future generations, like three rolls of panoramic photos of the Grand Canyon with nary a relative in sight.

Here are some suggestions for managing your surplus heirlooms:

1. Keep one small part of a large group, like a single place setting of china or one section of a deteriorated quilt, and display it.

2. Photograph or scan items before finding them a new home.

3. Document artifacts that shed light on a person's life before disposing of them. As you're culling your father's bookshelf, record the names of all the books before you sell or donate them. Describe a collection or group of photos, and how their existence reminds you of a special person's character. (Documenting artifacts is covered in more detail later in this chapter.)

4. Share the items with others who will treasure the legacy. This doesn't mean you should dump unwanted junk at your brother's house. But you could create a photo album for your brother from your duplicate photos or let him look through collections and pick out a few favorites to keep.

5. Sell a large-ticket item you don't need and use the proceeds to invest in your heritage. For example, sell Mom's fur coat at a consignment shop, then purchase a preservation kit for her wedding dress.

6. Donate an item to a cause your relative loved: Send your father's limited edition wildlife art print to the local humane society fundraiser.

7. Still can't part with it? Find a reason to keep it. Give it new life in your living space. Hang a textile, document, or other flat artifact on the wall. Start using Grandma's china. Give Dad's stamp collection to your son and help him add to it.

Document Your Heirlooms

After divesting yourself of extra stuff, you're ready to document the true treasures you've kept. You can do it quickly with a free Heirloom Inventory Form like the one found at *Family Tree Magazine*'s website **<www.familytreemagazine.com/FreeForms>**. A more thorough approach (which will be especially appreciated by loved ones when settling your estate) is to take pictures of your heirlooms and caption them with descriptions in photo albums, on scrapbook pages, or in the Family Heirlooms and Family Recipes sections of *Family Tree Memory Keeper* by Allison Stacy and Diane Haddad (Family Tree Books).

Remember, an unidentified heirloom will someday become just another garage sale trinket. It's the people and memories that make an object an heirloom. What should you identify about an heirloom?

» Provenance: Who and where it came from. Who made or purchased it originally? Why did they have it? Who else has owned it? How did it come to you? Give detailed explanations; include relatives' full names, where they lived, and other explanatory notes, like a profession or interest that led to them create or own the object.

» Documentation: You can more fully establish provenance by documenting your heirloom. Original receipts, the owner's manual, a letter mentioning the item, a photograph of the owner wearing it, etc.: All offer further evidence of the importance and authenticity of this heirloom to your personal or family story. If you have had an item professionally restored, repaired, etc., include reports from those who did the work.

» Stories and memories: Why is this heirloom valuable to you? Explain your sentimental attachment to the object. Write your memories and, as previously mentioned, place them in an album or binder along with photographs of the heirloom.

» Appraisal or other statement of financial value: Some items, by nature of their age and originality, have financial as well as sentimental value. If you have had an item appraised, include the appraiser's report. If an item has been insured, include the proper paperwork.

Preserve

As you take a closer look at your heirlooms, you may notice some in less-than-perfect condition. Of course, everything ages. Even items that look brand-new will gradually deteriorate. How they change depends both on the artifacts themselves (what they're made of) and how they're stored. Fortunately, you can slow down or minimize damage to your personal and family treasures.

The answer may be as simple as unfolding a blanket or moving a photograph out of direct sunlight. Other techniques require a little more investment of time, money, and research.

For items that are significantly damaged or appear to be actively deteriorating, consider consulting a conservator. Find one through groups such as the American Institute for Conservation of Historic and Artistic Works **<www.conservation-us.org>**. A conservator can use proven, minimally invasive methods to repair or restore an heirloom and advise you on proper storage materials and conditions for a particular type of material (silk, parchment, ivory, wood, etc.) or construction (embroidery, scrapbooks, furniture, etc.).

Take a close look at your heirlooms. Do they show breakage, crumbling, tearing, staining, fading, permanent crease marks, water or pest damage, etc.? Generally, if your document or other object is in good condition and doesn't seem to be actively deteriorating, you can preserve it as is by packing and storing it properly.

Pack Things Away

When it comes to packaging heirlooms for storage, use archival supplies purchased from a reputable vendor. These are pricier than your average manila file folder or cardboard box because they have extra manufacturing costs to remove acids and lignin. Acids are used in the paper-making process to break up wood fibers. Residues of those acids remain in ordinary paper and cardboard, and this residue makes paper deteriorate over time. *Lignin* is a natural plant polymer that's good for the living plant but causes slow chemical damage once the plant is made into paper. Archival-grade paper products have had most of the acid and lignin removed during manufacturing (watch for the terms *acid-free* and *lignin-free* on paper products, including boxes). Buffered paper and boxes contain an alkaline buffering agent that provides further safeguards against acids that remain in the paper. Archival boxes also are constructed with special adhesives that won't damage paper over time.

Some inert plastics are used in archival storage products, namely polyester (often known by popular brand names Mylar D or Melinex), polyethylene, and polypropylene. You'll find this material in plastic sleeves used to protect documents and photos. Polyvinyl acetate (PVA) is often used in conservation when adhesive is required. Be careful when choosing off-brand plastic products or those that don't specifically name the type of plastic used. A common plastic, polyvinyl chloride (PVC), emits damaging gases (ever smelled a new plastic shower curtain?) and is not safe for your heirloom storage.

Though some plastics can be used safely, avoid suffocating artifacts by sealing them entirely in airtight plastic containers. While this might seem a great solution for safely storing items in a damp basement, you'll also trap damaging moisture, gases, etc., *inside* the container.

Specific artifacts will respond best to specific storage products and methods. For example, buffered tissue, papers, and boxes should be used only with heirlooms made from plant-based materials (papers, undyed cotton, linen, etc.). Store paper and fabric items unfolded, or with as few folds as possible (refold them in a different direction every so often to prevent permanent creasing), with archival tissue cushioning the folds and hollows.

Try to preserve original order and grouping of documents and photos, as their positioning near each other may tell a story. Within the original order, separate different types of materials (news clippings, photos, etc.) from each other in archival sleeves to prevent acid and ink migration and other damage.

Learn more about archival techniques for specific materials in *Saving Stuff: How to Care for and Preserve*

Your Collectibles, Heirlooms, and Other Prized Possessions by Don Williams and Louisa Jagger; *Organizing and Preserving Your Heirloom Documents* by Katherine Scott Sturdevant, and the *Guide to Collections Care: Paper, Photographs, Textiles & Books*, a free brochure available from Gaylord Archival **<www.gaylord.com>**. Denise Levenick has written two titles for Family Tree Books on the subject of preservation, and these works are especially helpful: *How to Archive Your Family Keepsakes* (2012) and *How to Archive Family Photos* (2015). Both are available at **<www.shopfamilytree.com>**. Online, look to websites of reputed archiving sources such as The National Institute for Conservation **<www.heritagepreservation. org>**, The Smithsonian Museum Conservation Institute **<si.edu/mci>**, and various state or university archives. The Practical Archivist website **<practicalarchivist. com>**, hosted by professional archivist Sally Jacobs, also provides readable and fun insights on storing your family stuff.

A final word about choosing products: The term "archival" is not regulated. Neither are product descriptions like "great for photo storage." Choose products from vendors who have built their reputations on providing trustworthy supplies for archives, museums, and home archivists like you. See a partial list of these at the end of this chapter.

It won't do you any good to pamper your heirlooms in archival packaging if they are hidden away in musty basements, hot attics, or unregulated storage units. The rule of thumb is to store your treasures in the same conditions in which people like to live: moderate temperatures and low humidity. (Yes, this limits how much you can keep, unless your home has abundant closets or square footage.) Additionally, think about water pipes or other potentially harmful household objects near your heirlooms, even behind walls. Consider whether pests might be a problem; you don't want mice nesting in your wedding tux or bugs eating the bookbinding glue from your grandfather's diary. If you are going to display your items, keep them out of direct or strong light, and out of the reach of sticky fingers or curious cat paws.

Share with Family

We may safeguard heirlooms for our own enjoyment, but most of us have an eye to the future. We eventually want to share our stuff with loved ones. Passing on heirlooms can strengthen trust and understanding between family members. It perpetuates your legacy and can instill a sense of heritage in both young and old.

Lots of questions can surface when you start planning to share your heirlooms. Who should receive them? How do you divide a limited number of treasures among many relatives? Should you separate collections? What if you're not sure your mementoes will be sufficiently cared for or appreciated?

One way you can share family artifacts without having to part with them permanently is to put them on display in your home. When others visit, you can tell the stories behind them. There are some risks; artifacts might be damaged by exposure to everyday life. But you might deem that a small price to pay for the ability to enjoy and share your legacy any time while keeping it safe at home. Here are some suggestions for display:

1. Frame an antique photo, a small heirloom textile, or a copy of a family document or letter. Consult a professional framer for tips on framing these items without harming them. Hang these in areas that don't receive direct light, like hallways.

2. Arrange small mementoes or collections in a shadowbox frame, which is a deep frame that accommodates dimensional objects. Group objects to tell a story, like a rosary, missal, holy card, and photo of a First Communion, or a collection of trinkets from Grandpa's desk. A professional framer can help you mount some objects safely for vertical display (do not permanently adhere them to any surfaces). Otherwise, display your frame horizontally. Include a variety of sizes and materials for greater interest, and your handwritten or typed caption.

3. Include a conversation-starting artifact as part of your home's décor. Stack Grandpa's favorite books on a shelf with his spectacles perched on top; spread hand-stitched linen napkins on a sideboard or a home-spun quilt on a guest bed. Display linens only in little-used areas where damage is unlikely; try to display them unfolded.

4. Create an album of heirloom photos with detailed captions. Keep it out, like a coffee-table book, with every expectation of it being thumbed through. Be sure your album is made of archival materials and ensure that your photos are protected under clear archival pages.

When you are ready to part with heirlooms, consider both the artifact and the potential recipient. Chances are much better that your gift will be appreciated and well-cared for if given to someone who has shown interest in your family history, though certainly you can give heritage gifts in an effort to *awaken* interest. It's ideal if you can match a relative with an artifact he or she would love: an old tool, book, vintage jewelry, etc. Finally, consider whether the person has space, savvy, and likely willingness to care for an heirloom. If the person moves frequently or doesn't tend to keep items of sentimental value, you might first inquire before gifting a precious object.

Don't overlook the value of small, simple heir-looms—or what they might mean to a relative you don't know well. Your gifts don't need to be grand gestures. The littlest mementoes—a smooth glass bead, a watch fob, a business card—can become treasures simply for having belonged to an ancestor.

Once you've determined to give an heirloom gift, consider taking a few extra steps to ensure the gift can be appreciated for a long time. Many of the displays mentioned earlier make great gifts: anything in a frame, shadowbox, or another container. If you are giving a tex-tile or another fragile object, present it already wrapped in archival packaging. (Explain the packaging so the recipient doesn't throw away the tissues or boxes!) Don't forget that every heirloom gift should come with a written explanation of the object's provenance and significance to yourself and/or your family.

Old photos and documents are easy and inexpensive to copy and frame for more than one relative. Consider creating similar gifts—framed color copies of Grandma's watercolor paintings or a handsome display of family photos—for everyone at the holidays, especially when a family is large. When creating a photo display (particu-larly from different eras), consider printing all the images in black and white or sepia tone (browns) for a uniform, attractive look. Many basic photo editing software packages will do this for your digital images; be sure to preserve a digital image with its original coloring, too. If you have old family papers that aren't easy to copy, like a diary or faded letters, consider transcribing them into typed form. Create a binder or book for loved ones to enjoy. Add a description of those who penned the docu-ments and a photo of the authors if you have one.

Do you have some creative skills? Consider making over less-usable family artifacts into something new. A broken piece of furniture might be retooled into a walk-ing stick or a simple paperweight that shows the wood grain at its best. Your father's old ties or your mother's favorite floral shirts could be refashioned into a quilt or pillow (it might surprise you how well people recognize fabrics worn by their loved ones). Again, consider the objects and those who will receive them: What kind of gift would they appreciate?

Some family archivists wonder whether they should try to keep an heirloom collection intact or parcel it out among many relatives. The collection might be a full set of monogrammed china, folk art collected during a loved one's travels, or a more traditional stamp or coin collection. Consider whether the original owner would have wanted a painstakingly gathered collection of historic or cultural artifacts to remain together. If so, perhaps the most fitting legacy would be to donate the collection to an appropriate repository in the family member's name, and keep images of the items. If you care more about sharing these among your family members, document the collection as a whole before distributing it, and keep a record of what was distributed to whom.

Document collections often have the most historical and genealogical value when they remain together. Parceling out the ten love letters your grandparents wrote each other might please ten great-grandchildren, but their ability to tell your grandparents' stories lessens when the items are separated. Again, consider sharing copies, but try to keep original documents together.

Finally, think about your wishes for the heirlooms that remain in your possession during your lifetime. Mention important ones specifically in your will; indicate where they are in your home and who should receive them. Be sure the stories of these artifacts get passed along, either through letters included with your estate documents or in an heirloom inventory like the kinds previously mentioned (give your executor a copy of the heirloom log, or mention its location in your will). Not only will your heirlooms end up with the right people, your grieving relatives won't have the difficult and often tense experience of trying to divide family mementoes amongst themselves. Even when heirlooms are not specifically mentioned in your will, an accessible heirloom inventory may prevent your grandfather's quilt from being donated to the local thrift store.

It does take time, energy, and sometimes money to properly document, maintain, and distribute family heirlooms. But these artifacts were likely not accumulated in a day, and you don't need to have them all neatly wrapped up in a day, either. Just as you took the time to savor your memories as you told your stories in this book, take whatever time you can to savor—and save—the memories behind your meaningful possessions. Share them in any number of ways, but do share them somehow, so they can be heirlooms in someone else's life someday, continuing the task of reminding that person of his or her legacy just as the items have for you.

Archival Products Vendors

» Archival Products
  <www.archival.com>
  800-526-5640

» Gaylord Archival
  <www.gaylord.com>
  800-962-9580

» Hollinger Metal Edge
  <www.hollingermetaledge.com>
  800-634-0491

» Talas
  <www.talasonline.com>
  212-219-0770

» University Products
  <www.universityproducts.com>
  800-628-1912

10

special forms

Special People

_____

Name _____

Relationship _____

About this person and our relationship: _____
_____
_____
_____
_____
_____
_____
_____
_____

What this person has meant to me: _____
_____
_____
_____
_____
_____
_____
_____
_____
_____

Special People

Name _____

Relationship _____

About this person and our relationship: _____

_____

_____

_____

_____

_____

_____

_____

_____

_____

_____

What this person has meant to me: _____

_____

_____

_____

_____

_____

_____

_____

_____

_____

_____

Special Places

AS REMEMBERED BY _____

Honor a particular place that has been meaningful to you, whether it was an entire city or your grandparents' back porch.

Name of Place _____

Location _____

Write a description of this place. _____

_____

_____

_____

_____

_____

_____

_____

Why was this place was special to you? _____

_____

_____

_____

_____

_____

_____

_____

_____

_____

_____

Special Places

AS REMEMBERED BY _____

Honor a particular place that has been meaningful to you, whether it was an entire city or your grandparents' back porch.

Name of Place _____

Location _____

Write a description of this place. _____

_____

_____

_____

_____

_____

_____

_____

Why was this place was special to you? _____

_____

_____

_____

_____

_____

_____

_____

_____

_____

_____

Special Memories

Event_____

Date/Time Period _____

Location _____

Write your memory. Tell who was involved and describe what you were doing. Use full names and specific details. _____

_____

_____

_____

_____

_____

_____

_____

_____

Why is this memory so special to you? _____

_____

_____

_____

_____

_____

_____

_____

_____

_____

Special Memories

AS REMEMBERED BY _____

Event _____

Date/Time Period _____

Location _____

Write your memory. Tell who was involved and describe what you were doing. Use full names and specific details. _____

_____

_____

_____

_____

_____

_____

_____

_____

Why is this memory so special to you? _____

_____

_____

_____

_____

_____

_____

_____

_____

_____

Life-Changing Experiences

AS REMEMBERED BY _____

Event _____

Date/Time Period _____

Location _____

Write your memories of this experience. Who was involved and what happened? Use specific details.

_____

_____

_____

_____

_____

_____

_____

_____

_____

_____

How did this experience change the way you thought or felt or lived your life? Use specific details: what you thought or felt, or the differences you noticed in yourself. _____

_____

_____

_____

_____

_____

_____

_____

_____

_____

Flashbulb Memories

Your vivid recollection of a highly public event, like a natural or man-made disaster or the assassination of a public figure.

_____

Public Event   Date

Where were you when you heard about this public event? _____

_____

_____

_____

How did you hear about it? _____

_____

_____

_____

How did you react? How did others around you react? _____

_____

_____

_____

What images, sounds, or other details do you remember about that day? _____

_____

_____

_____

Did your life change (or a loved one's life) in consequence of this important event? _____

_____

_____

_____

_____

Memorabilia

Adhere copies of important documents, photos, postcards, or other memorabilia to this page. Insert a copy of this page in the appropriate section of your book. Do not adhere original documents, photographs, or other valuable one-of-a-kind materials to this page. Those should be stored in an archival environment.

Describe the item featured on this page, its significance, and the location of the original if the item is a copy.

_____

_____

_____

_____

_____

_____

_____

_____

_____

_____

_____

Memorabilia

Adhere copies of important documents, photos, postcards, or other memorabilia to this page. Insert a copy of this page in the appropriate section of your book. Do not adhere original documents, photographs, or other valuable one-of-a-kind materials to this page. Those should be stored in an archival environment.

Describe the item featured on this page, its significance, and the location of the original if the item is a copy.

_____

_____

_____

_____

_____

_____

_____

_____

_____

_____

_____

In Memoriam

On a Memorabilia page, attach a copy of a funeral card, obituary, photo of a tombstone, or another memento relating to this person's passing.

In Memory of _____

Relationship to You _____

Date and Place of Death _____

Circumstances and/or Cause of Death _____

Location of Funeral _____

Location of Burial/Cremation _____

Describe the last memorable time you spent with this person. _____

_____

_____

_____

_____

Write some thoughts or feelings about this person, or about losing this person. _____

_____

_____

_____

_____

_____

What do you wish you could tell or ask this person? _____

_____

_____

_____

_____

_____

ABOUT THE AUTHOR

Sunny Morton is an award-winning writer who has advanced training in genealogy, history, and memoir-writing. She is a contributing editor for *Family Tree Magazine* and Lisa Louise Cooke's *Genealogy Gems*, and is also a writing coach for Family Tree University. Learn more about her at <www.sunnymorton.com>.

ISBN: 978-1-4403-4714-6

Other Family Tree Books are available from your local bookstore and online suppliers. For more genealogy resources, visit <shopfamilytree.com>.

22 21 20 19   9 8 7 6

DISTRIBUTED IN THE U.K. AND EUROPE BY

F&W Media International, LTD

Brunel House, Forde Close,

Newton Abbot, TQ12 4PU, UK

Tel: (+44) 1626 323200,

Fax (+44) 1626 323319

E-mail: enquiries@fwmedia.com

fw

a content + ecommerce company

PUBLISHER AND COMMUNITY LEADER: Allison Dolan

EDITOR: Andrew Koch

DESIGNER: Julie Barnett

PRODUCTION COORDINATOR: Debbie Thomas

4 FREE
FAMILY TREE
templates

- decorative family tree posters
- five-generation ancestor chart
- family group sheet
- bonus relationship chart
- type and save, or print and fill out

Download at <ftu.familytreemagazine.com/free-family-tree-templates>

MORE GREAT GENEALOGY RESOURCES

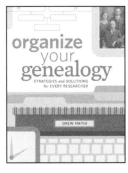

FAMILY TREE MEMORY KEEPER

By the Editors of Family Tree Magazine

HOW TO ARCHIVE FAMILY PHOTOS

By Denise Levenick

ORGANIZE YOUR GENEALOGY

By Drew Smith

Available from your favorite bookstore, online booksellers and **<shopfamilytree.com>**, or by calling (855) 278-0408.

 Join our community! <facebook.com/familytreemagazine>